Psalms/Now

Psalms/Now

Leslie F. Brandt

CONCORDIA PUBLISHING HOUSE · SAINT LOUIS

Reprinted 2003 Concordia Publishing House
Copyright ©1974, 1996 Concordia Publishing House
3558 S. Jefferson Avenue, St. Louis, MO 63118-3968

Manufactured in the United States of America

Library of Congress Cataloging-in-Publication Data

Brandt, Leslie F.
    Psalms/now / Leslie F. Brandt.
    p.   cm.

    1. Bible. O.T. Psalms—Paraphrases, English. I. Title.
BS1440.B73   1996
223'.205209—dc20 96-14857

---

6 7 8 9 10 11 12 13   10 09 08 07 06 05 04 03

Foreword

The Book of Psalms is a miniature Bible, a miniature
history of God's people. It expresses all the feelings and
experiences they will ever have.

John F. Brug
People's Bible Commentary: Psalms II

Perhaps the best-known and best-loved book of the Bible,
the Psalms have long held a central position in the spiritual life of
believers. From the original authors to the modern reader, the
Psalms express our emotions, our desires, even our faith, to our
heavenly Father. As one person has said, "We were born with this
book in our very bones."[1]

Originally written as personal or community expressions of
worship, countless generations have used the Psalms to convey "the
whole range of human emotions in their relation to God, from
extreme pessimism and doubt to simple and certain trust."[2] Psalms
were assigned for each Jewish festival and temple ritual. Some of
these prayer-poems may have been written for the coronation cere-
monies of the Israelite kings. Other psalms were much more private,
communicating personal, heartfelt needs, sorrows, or joys. Every
possible human experience and emotion is addressed in this book of
150 poems, including salvation, bondage, illness, healing, birth,
death, joy, depression, anger, and thankfulness. And the list grows
with each new reading and each new life event.

The child Jesus probably first heard and learned the psalms
from His parents and then continued to study them as an integral
part of His formal education in the synagogue. The New Testament
indicates that Jesus and the apostles were well-versed in the
Psalter—the most-quoted Old Testament book in the New
Testament. In fact, the disciples and Jesus probably sang psalms

often—even on the night Jesus was betrayed (Mark 14:26). The apostle Paul instructs the early Christians to include the psalms in their worship (see 1 Corinthians 14:15, 26; Ephesians 5:19; Colossians 3:16). Today, we continue to use the psalms for public worship (as litanies, Scripture readings, prayers, and in hymn form) and for private devotions.

But why have such statements as "The Lord is my shepherd" or "God is our refuge and strength" or "Create in me a pure heart, O God" remained timely for the modern reader? How can these ancient songs of praise, petition, lament, and joy still be relevant? Perhaps it's because the Hebrew writers communicated a depth of emotion with which we all can identify. William Swan Plumer, a 19th-century clergyman and Bible scholar, found that, when his spirit was "excited, or devotional, or sad, and [seeking] an echo to its enthusiasm, its devotion, or its melancholy," he turned to the Psalms.

> There I find words which seem to issue from the soul of the ages, and which penetrate even to the heart of all generations. ... Read Greek or Latin poetry after a Psalm, and see how pale it looks.[3]

When God's Holy Spirit directs our reading and studying of the Psalms, we see reflected back to us the sin that separates us from God (Psalm 51) and God's perfect plan of salvation fulfilled in Jesus that erases that sin and binds us to Him (Psalm 22). While Martin Luther first realized the truth of justification by faith from his study of Romans, his study of the Psalter reinforced his new understanding of the "righteousness of God" (Psalm 85).

Luther came to see the righteousness of God not as the threat of God's righteous judgment against sinners but as God's grace and mercy in Christ. "The 'righteousness of God' is that through which the righteous lives by the gift of God ... through which the merciful God justifies us by faith."[4] Thus, Luther found that all the Scriptures point-ed to the sweet Gospel message that God has worked salvation for us and gives it freely.

Luther found in the Psalms strength and inspiration for his struggle with the Roman Catholic Church. He and his circle of friends often sang Psalm 46 when feeling overwhelmed. Indeed this psalm, on which Luther based the Reformation anthem "A Mighty Fortress Is Our God," is known as the psalm of "holy confidence" for God's people.[5] Luther not only found inspiration in the Psalms for many of his hymns, he spent significant time studying them, lecturing on them, and reading them for his own spiritual growth. Luther commented:

BRANDT'S POETIC RESTATEMENTS OF THE PSALMS EXPLORE OUR CONTEMPORARY RELATIONSHIP TO GOD.

> With this book I have occupied, delighted, and trained myself from my youth, and, thanks be to God, not without great benefit. Yea, I would not exchange the blessing of the Holy Spirit which I have obtained by enjoying and considering the psalms for all the thrones and kingdoms of this world. [6]

Another explanation for our love of the Psalms may exist in Jesus' love for the Psalms. The Gospels record numerous references to the Psalms. At His baptism, the voice from heaven echoed the words of Psalm 2:7, "You are My Son; today I have become Your Father." Several Beatitudes find their beginnings in the Psalms (for example, "Blessed are the meek" echoes Psalm 37:11). The crowds that welcomed Jesus to Jerusalem before His death cried out "Blessed is He who comes in the name of the Lord!" (Psalm 118:26). As Jesus hung on the cross, He cried out "My God, My God, why have You forsaken Me?" (Psalm 22:1). And after His resurrection, Jesus opened the minds of His disciples to understand how all Scripture, including the Psalms, pointed to Him as the Christ, the promised Messiah (see Luke 24:27, 45–47).

Peter quoted the Psalms in his great Pentecost sermon (Acts 2:25–28, 34–35). And the early church leaders continued to incorporate the Psalms in their worship, always reading them with a messianic ear. In these ancient songs, the new believers found the truth of God's promises in Jesus Christ.

We only need to look at one psalm, Psalm 23, to see how central the entire book is to our spiritual life. As one commentator says:

> This Psalm has sung its way into more hearts than any other part of the Bible except the Lord's Prayer. ... The tiny tot memorizes it before he can read, and the old man dies with it upon his lips.[9]

And William Plumer adds his admiration for the poet King David as he asks, "Where else do we find a whole Psalm expressive of personal confidence, joy, and triumph from beginning to end?"[8]

If the Psalms are the "faith of the Old Testament set to music,"[9] then Psalm 23 is the apex of this Old Testament hymnal. Here David carries his praise beyond thankfulness for a specific act of salvation to "a confession that God will always exercise personal care ... . The psalmist ... does not simply pray for this but claims the certainty of enjoying it."[10] In Jesus' words that He is the Good Shepherd, we come full circle to realize that God has delivered us from the evils of sin and this world and leads us to quiet waters and green pastures. From its first singing until the present, Psalm 23 "has dried many tears and supplied the mould into which many hearts have poured their peaceful faith."[11] Psalm 23 will continue to uplift believers and provide the assurance that God does walk with us, even carry us, until we reach His eternal banquet table.

If the original Psalms are still speaking to today's Christians, why do we need a paraphrase such as *Psalms/Now*? Because this paraphrase provides Christians with new ways to celebrate the promises of protection, victory, salvation, light, and life God offers us through the words of the Psalms. Brandt's poetic restatements of the Psalms, rooted in the emotions and faith of the ancient songs, explore our contemporary relationship to God. These modern poems help us understand that we can, in our own everyday language, praise God, plead with God, question God, even yell at God.

Brandt says in his preface that he has spent years reading the Psalms, finding in them ways to "articulat[e] my feelings and verbaliz[e] my prayers as a struggling saint." He has offered this paraphrase as one way to "honestly and openly express ... doubts and perplexities to the living God" so we can "lay claim to God's promises and demonstrate our faith." These are the very things the original psalm writers sought. Their songs expressed the depth of their emotions and faith in their heavenly Father.

The Psalms, whether in a "modern" paraphrase or the original, should have a distinct place in our devotional life, a place that reflects their witness to Christ as Lord and Savior and their remarkable "capacity to express the character of the individual's relationship to God."[12] Each of us can, as Brandt has, adapt the Psalms to address our own joys and concerns. Using the biblical text as a guide, we can give voice to our personal prayers and praises and give God the glory due His name. And in those moments when words fail us, we can call to mind the soft reminder that the Lord is our Shepherd, the sweet assurance that His love endures forever, and then join "everything that has breath" in praise of our great God.

The Editor

1. A. Chouraqui as quoted in *The Psalms: A New Translation* (Westminister Press, 1963).

2. J. W. Rogerson and J. W. McKay, *The Cambridge Bible Commentary: Psalms 1–50.* (Cambridge, Great Britain: Cambridge University Press, 1977), 2.

3. William Swan Plumer as quoted in *The Treasury of David*, Volume 3, by Charles Hadden Spurgeon. (Grand Rapids: Zondervan, 1966), 465.

4. Ewald M. Plass, comp., *What Luther Says*. (St. Louis: Concordia, 1959), 1226.

5. Debb Andrus, comp., *God's Word for Today: Psalms*. (St. Louis: Concordia, 1994), 11–12.

6. Martin Luther as quoted in *Studies in the Psalter*, by O. W. Wismar. (St. Louis: Concordia, 1926), 1.

7. Arnold B. Rhodes, *The Layman's Bible Commentary: The Book of Psalms*. (Richmond: John Knox Press, 1960), 51.

8. William Swan Plumer as quoted in *The Treasury of David*, Volume 1, by Charles Hadden Spurgeon. (Grand Rapids: Zondervan, 1966), 357–358.

9. Rhodes, 8.

10. Patrick D. Miller Jr., *Interpreting the Psalms*. (Philadelphia: Fortress Press, 1986), 119 (emphasis added).

11. A. Cohen, *The Psalms*. (London: The Soncino Press, 1950), 67.

12. Miller, 21.

Preface

I first read the Book of Psalms through at the age of 10.
I don't remember what they said to me at that time, but in the
ensuing years they often articulated my feelings and verbalized my
prayers as a struggling saint. In the 20th year of my ordained min-
istry, I began to "rewrite" a few of them for my church bulletin.
These were eventually published in three small volumes and later
were all included in a single book, *Psalms/Now*. Now, more than
20 years later, this present volume has been revised. The language
speaks to both young and old, male and female, longtime Christian
and newcomer to the faith.

I am expressing what the Old Testament psalmists might be
saying if they were approaching the 21st century. The name *Christ*
is not used; the Messianic import of the Old Testament psalms is
not noted. Yet these prayers are voiced by those on the Christian
side of the Easter event—believers whose every approach to God
must be by way of God revealed through Jesus Christ.

Today's Christians, like the ancient psalmists, can honestly and
openly express their doubts and perplexities to the living God. And
as we do this, we can lay claim to God's promises and demonstrate
our faith in celebration of His presence in the world today. If these
psalm-writing efforts help make the ancient psalms more relevant
for modern saints and if they help express more adequately the
perpetual conflicts of a child of God in our complex society, they
will serve their purpose.

Leslie F. Brandt, 1996

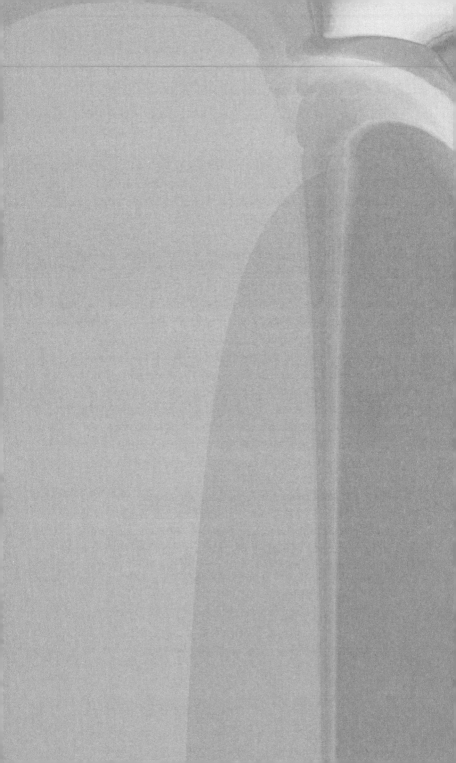

Those persons who choose to live significant lives
   are not going to take their cues
      from the religiously indifferent.
Nor will they conform to the crowd
   nor mouth their prejudices
      nor dote on the failures of others.

Their ultimate concern is the will of God.
They make their daily decisions in respect to such.
Compare them to a sturdy tree
   planted in rich, moist soil.
As the tree yields fruit,
   so their lives manifest blessing for others
      and are purposeful and productive.

This is not true concerning the ungodly.
They are like sand in a desert storm
   or leaves in an autumn wind.
They cannot stand against the judgments
   of the eternal God.
And they are most uncomfortable
   among those who demonstrate genuine faith
      in the God of righteousness.

The children of God walk in the course
   that God has ordained.
The children of unbelief walk
   in paths of self-destruction.

2

Why do dictators and governments
    throughout our world
    persist in persecuting the people of God?
They may be divided in everything else,
    but they unite in their endeavors
    to free themselves from the restraints of religion.

Disconcerting as this is to me,
    our great God laughs at their foolish efforts.
And His laughter will have the sound of fury
    in the day He determines to act against them.
He will reveal to them who truly is Lord and King.

But to me, even in the midst of my confusion,
    He speaks as a loving Father.
"You are My child and servant," God says.
"Trust in Me; I control the
    destiny of the world.
You shall overcome;
    you shall frustrate their attempts to destroy you."

So wise up, you who sit in high places.
Begin serving the God you are trying to silence.
Bow your hearts in submission
    before He crowns your heads with divine wrath.
Only those who rest in God's will are truly secure.

3

O God, so many obstacles confront me today!
And even as they press in upon me,
  there are people around me
    who laugh at my childlike dependence on You.
They claim that my faith is futile,
  that God is not interested in my petty problems.

But, God, You have surrounded me with Your love.
You envelop me with concern
  and undergird me with grace.
When I reach out for You,
  You are close enough to hear and to respond.

Whether I am awake or asleep,
  You are near me and watch over me.
I do not have to be afraid
  of these problems that assail me.
The conflicts of my life will not separate me from You.

I constantly seek Your deliverance
  from all that hurts or hinders.
You are able to rid my life of everything
  that may threaten my relationship with You.
You will, in Your own good time, set me free
  from every human fault and frailty.
But even while I await Your ultimate deliverance,
  help me sense Your presence and power
    in the midst of my many conflicts.

4

Dear God, respond to Your servant in distress;
　　make room for a disciple in despair;
　　listen to the agonizing cries of a child
　　　　who is depressed and unhappy.
O you who I thought were my friends,
　　why do you keep hacking at me,
　　　　gloating over my errors,
　　　　rejoicing at my failures,
　　　　always looking for the very worst in me?

I must remember that I truly do belong to God,
　　that He does feel for me when I hurt.

Go ahead, explode, cry out, or complain;
　　it doesn't frighten God,
　　　　but guard that you don't hurt anyone else.
Then, O foolish heart, simmer down
　　and renew your confidence in God.

I hear voices around me
　　whining about the wickedness of the world,
　　begging for divine demonstration of might and right.
And yet I know I have discovered
　　more delight in my relationship with You, O Lord,
　　than they in all their possessions and pleasures.

And so I can lie down and sleep in peace.
Because of You, I am eternally secure.

Can You hear, O God, what I have to say?
Do You feel something of what I feel this morning?

I know, O God, that You are grieved
   by the selfishness of Your children.
The world You created seems to be falling apart.
Your creatures are living for themselves alone,
   proud and self-sufficient.
They think they don't need You any longer.
I also know, O Lord, that I cannot exist
   without the assurance of Your eternal love.
Thus I commit myself once more to You and Your purposes.
Help me walk in Your path for my life.
Give me grace to overcome the many obstacles.

The philosophies that come out of our world
   bear little resemblance
      to the truth You revealed to us.
These subtle, seductive worldviews
   lead people astray
      through forked tongues and suave soft-sell.
Enable us to recognize them for what they are:
   shallow, superficial, ultimately destructive.

Those who follow You need not be dismayed.
They can sing and dance in the joy of their Lord.
You will continue to reveal Yourself to them
   and care for them and work out Your purposes
      in and through them.

6

O God, don't clobber me in disgust
or chastise me in anger.
But the fact is, I'm falling apart.
I am distraught and confused.
I am in deep trouble,
and I don't know how long I can take it.

I can only beg You to enter into my conflict,
to extricate me from this incessant battering,
to demonstrate Your love
in deliverance and salvation.
Otherwise I'm going down the drain;
and how, then, could I either praise or serve You?

I am fed up with this continual agony;
I can no longer endure these perpetual defeats.
I am becoming increasingly discouraged
about my human frailties and fallibilities.

If only I could be sure
that You know about my anguish,
that You discern my cries for help,
that You also feel and understand,
that You will never let me go.
Then I could stand firm even in defeat
and rise victorious even over my failures
and make even my human weaknesses
serve You.

O God, I come running to You
	like a frightened child.
My pursuers, like hideous monsters,
	seek to tear me limb from limb.

O Lord,
	if I really am to blame for their hostilities,
	if I have willfully hurt anybody,
	if I have selfishly blighted another person's soul,
		then let the ax fall;
	I have no right to live;
		I almost wish I could die.

O God, have mercy.
You know the secrets of my heart
	and the desires of my flesh.
You know I want so much to do Your will.
You know my greatest enemy is myself,
	how ineffectual I am
		in dealing with my inner conflicts.
You know, and You have assured me, that You care.
You have judged my wickedness;
	now rise up to deliver me
		from its ugly consequences.

Oh, when will there be an end to evil?
When will this frustrating struggle cease?
I claw like a wounded animal
	at the promises of God for comfort.

I appeal to His love for solace and strength.

I know the end of those
    who do not repent of their sins.
Their selfishness boomerangs; sin kicks back.
They stew in their own juices.

Thus I must run to God in my defeats
    that I may learn to walk with Him in His victories.
I will continue to sing His praises
    and to lay claim to His righteousness.

8

O God,
    how full of wonder and splendor You are!

I see the reflections of Your beauty
    and hear the sounds of Your majesty
        wherever I turn.

Even the babbling of babes
    and the laughter of children
        spell out Your name in indefinable syllables.

When I gaze into star-studded skies
    and attempt to comprehend the vast distances,
I contemplate in utter amazement
    my Creator's concern for me.
I am dumbfounded that You
    should care personally about me.

And yet You have made me in Your image.
You have called me Your child
    and chosen me to be Your servant.
You have assigned to me
    the fantastic responsibility
        of carrying on Your creative activity.

O God,
    how full of wonder and splendor You are!

9

My heart overflows with gratitude to God.
I feel so exuberant,
>I simply must express or explode.
I will give voice to my exaltations;
>I will sing Your praises, O my God.

You helped me stand firm
>despite those who had it in for me,
and they were not successful
>in their efforts to discredit me.

You have destroyed great forces
>that rose up to oppose You throughout the ages.
You continue to rule over our fractured world,
>to sit in judgment over its nations and peoples.
You offer Your strong hand to those who are oppressed,
>Your loving concern to those who are troubled.
You never hide from those who seek You
>or forsake those who cling to You.

Sing the praises of God;
>proclaim loudly His deeds to the people.
For while He judges evildoers,
>He hears and remembers the cries of those in distress.

I always need Your gracious love.
You know all about my inner fears and doubts.
You hold me back from the brink of destruction.

You make it possible for me to sing Your praises
and to rejoice in Your perpetual deliverance.

Ungodly nations sink in their own sewage.
Men and women who promote evil
snare themselves in their own nets,
but those who recognize their need of You
shall be found by You.

Is it any wonder
my heart overflows with gratitude to God?

10

Where in the world are You hiding, O God?
Why are You not available when things go wrong?

The sensualist lives by the desires of the flesh.
The materialist seeks temporal security alone.
The ungodly person indulges in self-worship
and assumes that God is dead.

The point is, these are the ones who seem to prosper.
They laugh in scorn at those inclined toward piety.
They claim that they are in the driver's seat
and cannot be dethroned.
They live and speak arrogantly and carelessly.
They lack concern for the enslaved and the deprived.
They take what they want
without thought for the hurt they cause others.

Wake up, O God! Come out of hiding!
How can You allow these God-defiers to get away with it?

O God, You do take note of those in conflict.
You will take account of the godless and the arrogant.
You are still Lord over all the world.
You do hear the cries of those who love You;
You are continuously concerned about their needs.
You will enable them to stand
against the oppression and pain of this life.

I am frightened by the insecurities around me.
I am sorely tempted to run for my life,
    to take refuge in foolish escapades
        that dim the vision and drug the soul.

There is no escape
    from the realities of this fractured world.
When we awaken from our stupor
    or return to sobriety,
    they are ever present
        to haunt and oppress us.

But there is a place of refuge.
God is in our midst.
He is aware of the fears and apprehensions
    of His beloved children.
He may not always rid us of our fears.
But He does promise to face them with us,
    to make them stepping-stones to faith,
        to use them to draw us closer to Himself.

I need not worry too much
    about the distortions of this world.
I do need to be aware that God is here
    and trust that, through me,
        He will reveal Himself to His world.

O God, help me.
The world is truly going to the dogs.
Infidelity and deceit surround me.
Every person seems to wear two faces.

And people even boast about their deeds of evil.
They assume that they can talk themselves
     out of any corner.
They defy authority and live for themselves alone.

Our God will not remain silent forever.
His voice like thunder will drown out
       the foolish boasts of His unfaithful creatures.
"The maligned and the deprived
       have suffered long enough," He will say.
"I will rise to their defense
       and grant them My protection."
And what God promises, He will do.

Keep us, great God, from the indecision and
       vile compromises of this
           valueless generation.

O God, sometimes You seem so far away.
I cannot in this moment sense Your presence
 or feel Your power.

The darkness enveloping me is stifling.
This depression is suffocating.
How long, O God, do I have to live in this void?
O God, how long?

Break into this black night, O God;
 fill in this vast emptiness.
Enter into my conflict
 lest I fall, never to rise again.

I continue to trust in Your ever-present love.
I shall again discover true joy
 in my relationship with You.
I will proclaim Your praises, my Lord,
 for You will never let me go.

14

How foolish it is to deny the existence of God
or to say that God is dead!
And yet many do so.
They say it in the way they live
if not in the words they speak.

Our great God is forever searching for those
who live their lives for Him.
He is not looking for
verbal professions alone
but active, living testimonies of faith.

He sees denial and rebellion in the lives of all people.
What good they do is tainted by sin and self-centeredness.
They are more apt to be destructive than creative.
How foolish they are
to neglect God!

It is obvious that God works
through those who trust Him,
through those who dedicate their lives
to His service.
It is they who are set free from self-glory
to enjoy and to serve the living God.
They truly celebrate the eternal presence of God.

_15_

Who is the one, O Lord, that demonstrates
   participation in Your kingdom?
What are the prerequisites
   for membership in Your family?

Your child, O Lord, walks cautiously—
   and in obedience to Your precepts and principles.
He is open and honest before God and people.
She speaks and acts in love toward her neighbor.
He cannot condone that which is evil
   and doesn't participate
      in that which promotes injustice.
She listens to her sister's griefs
   and complaints.
He seeks to lighten his brother's burden
   and to share in his sorrow and pain.
She reaches out to heal rather than to hurt,
   to be kind and gentle to all who cross her path.

Those who demonstrate this loving relationship
   with God and His human creatures
   manifest participation in His kingdom.
They will never be separated from the family of God.

16

Sustain me, O God,
   for my faith is anchored in You.
I say it again,
      "You are my Lord;
      when I am estranged from You,
      I have nothing that is of any real worth."

The significant and contributive people
      of this world know You.
I must respect these individuals.
Those who make lesser things their ultimate concern
      are investing in eventual trouble and grief.
I cannot worship their idols
      or respect their objectives.

God has become my ultimate concern.
He is the Pilot of my ship.
Thus the course before me will lead
      to ultimate fulfillment.
I am guaranteed an inheritance of infinite value.

I look to God as my chief counselor.
Even in the darkest night,
      He is ready to teach and guide me.
Because He continually surrounds me,
      I shall not lose my way.

Is it any wonder that I am happy?

Even my humanity, my tangible body,
    rests in the blessed realization of this security.
God will keep even my human self
    from the destructive clutch of evil.

You do show me the paths I must take, O Lord.
Within Your all-embracing presence
    lies genuine fulfillment.
In my relationship with You,
    I discover incomparable and eternal joy.

17

I cry to You out of desperation, my God.
Listen to me and judge me if I am in error.

I have honestly tried to do Your will,
    to promote Your causes, to speak Your Word.
I have avoided the pitfalls that have victimized
    so many around me.
I have acted in love rather than in anger.
I have never raised my hand in violence.
I have walked in the paths You have set before me.

And yet despair trips me up.
There are great walls that I cannot break through,
    dead ends that lead nowhere,
        people to whom I cannot relate.
I reach out in concern and am rebuked with scorn.

I am weary, Lord, weary of well-doing.
I am tired of the reactions
    of those I seek to serve.
I seriously wonder if it is all worth it.

Grant me, O God, a measure of heavenly joy.
Help me feel good about myself
    and about my role in Your service.
Reveal Yourself in some special way this night
    that I may rest in joy and peace.

It is no wonder that I love You, O God.
You have granted me a security
   that I could never find
      among the things of this world.

You have erased from my life the fear of death.
What follows the grave no longer causes fearful concern.
The traumatic experiences of this life
   cannot destroy me.
You are never out of reach
   but are ever aware of my problems and conflicts.

How great and all-powerful is my God!
      The quaking of the earth,
      the shaking of the mountains,
      the blackness of the night,
      the beauty of the heavens,
      the lightning that crisscrosses the skies,
      the oceans that lash against the shores,
      this and much more bears witness
         to the majesty of my God.
And this is the God who is concerned about me.
He reaches into my distraught life
   to heal my wounds.
He encompasses me with eternal love.
He abides with me
   even in the midst of conflict or calamity.
He sets me free from self-idolatry

so I may serve His creatures around me.
He shields me from the forces that are intent
      on my destruction.
It is no wonder, O God, that I love You.

Can there be any God but this God that I love?
He surrounds me with His strength
      and clothes me with His grace.
He puts into my hands gifts to relay to others.
He entrusts me with tasks
        far beyond my human abilities
      and enables me to carry them out.
He ordains me as His child and servant,
        destined to accomplish His purposes
          among the peoples of this world.

Thus I celebrate God's presence
      in my life and world.
God is not dead; He lives!
I rejoice in His concern and love for me.
I will proclaim, O Lord,
      Your praises to anyone who will listen.
I will sing and shout and dance
      in the joy of knowing that You are my God.

Wherever I am, wherever I go,
I can sense something of the power of God.
The grandeur of the mountains,
the vastness of the oceans,
the breathtaking wonder of interstellar space;
all this proclaims the glory and majesty of God.
Even amid the clutter of our cities,
built and abused by our hands,
there are reflections of divine splendor.
God's voice can be heard.
He makes His presence known throughout the world.

God has made a path on which we are to walk.
In His will there is order and purpose.
He has proclaimed and demonstrated eternal truth
through the lips and lives of His children.
There are set before men and women precepts
and principles that direct God's creatures
in the way of peace and joy.
He has given meaning to life,
goals and objectives to this existence.
Therein is the answer to our inner need,
the fulfillment of our deepest longings.
These things are more precious and of greater
value than anything we could ever experience
or even dare to imagine.

This is the course which I must travel.
It is not easy; I make so many mistakes.

Faults and obsessions plague me.
O God, forbid that these should destroy me.
Set me free from their tenacious hold.
Encompass me with Your love and grace
    that these things may not stand
        between You and me.

O God,
    these are the thoughts
        that crowd my heart today.
Accept them and respond to them.
Enable me to realize anew
    the security and serenity
    of Your loving presence in my life.

O my very dear friend.
How much I want to bear your burden,
      to share your trouble!
But I can only pray that God may be
      very close to you in your sorrow
      and keep you and protect you in your conflict.
May He remember that you are His own,
      that you have dedicated your life to Him,
      that your heart's desire is to serve and please Him.
May He reach out to touch you and heal you;
      May He fulfill your crying need in this hour.
And may we soon rejoice together over His deliverance
      and walk together in His service.

I know that God does stand by His own.
Our failures do not stay His loving hand.
He transforms them into victories.
People around us put their trust in science and money,
      but such will fail to solve
            the real problems of our lives.
It is only in the name of God
      that we who fall can find the grace to rise again.

Hear my prayer on behalf of my friend, O God.
I want to share in my friend's pain and defeat;
      may I also share in my friend's joy and victory.

21

O God,
   in the grace and strength that You grant daily,
      Your servant finds reason for celebration.
You have truly fulfilled my innermost longings.
You have responded to my deepest needs.

I asked for security,
   and You encompassed me with love.
I looked to You for life,
   and You granted me life everlasting.
I sought identity,
   and You adopted me as Your child.
Whatever is of value and worth in my life
   has come through Your rich blessings.
My heart is glad in the realization
   of Your eternal presence.
I know that I will never lose Your love.

I raise my voice in praise, O God,
   because no one can separate me from You.
Although circumstances threaten me
      and my own obsessions entangle me,
   You will never let me go.
Your great power is sufficient to set me free
   from these things that hurt my soul.
I put my trust in You;
   You will not let them destroy me.
I find so many reasons for praising You, O God.

O God, why have You left me?
Why are You so far from me?
I can no longer feel You near.
I reach desperately for You,
     but I cannot find You.

I know You are holy and all-righteous
     and everywhere present.
The saints of past years believed in You
     and trusted You.
You responded to their cries.
They sought You, and they found You.
It is no wonder that Your praises
     were constantly on their lips.

But I feel as empty and insignificant
     as a bag full of wind.
I don't really expect people's plaudits,
     but I so sorely feel their criticisms.
I risk all in following
          what I feel to be Your will for me;
          yet even my friends fail to support me,
          and they actually turn against me.
"He thinks he's doing God's will," they say.
"But he'll be sorry he made that decision."

I believe that You have been with me
     from the very beginning of my life.

I know that You have cared for me
　　through these many years.
But, God, I need You now.
I am in trouble,
　　and I can't find You or feel You near.
At this moment, I feel as if I am falling apart.
Nothing seems to make sense anymore.
Everything I attempt ends in failure.
I feel inferior and weak.
Those I have tried to serve
　　are actually gloating
　　　　over my flops and failures.
I know, O God, that much of it
　　is a matter of my foolish feelings.
The fact is, You are not far off.
You know both my feelings and my failings.
Yet You love me and accept me.
You will save me—even from myself.

Thus I will continue to sing Your praises.
In spite of or in scorn of my feelings,
　　I will celebrate Your loving presence.
As despicable as I may feel at times,
　　You do not despise me. Neither will You leave me.
Your love is personal, and it is eternal.

Nor will You despise or ignore the afflictions

that plague Your many sons and daughters.
Your children and servants are precious to You.
Even when they fail You, You never fail them.
You hear their cries and feel their pain
	and are ever ready to support them
		in their conflicts.

I dedicate myself anew to You, O Lord.
I will serve You
	whatever the cost or the consequence.
You are my God.
Regardless of my feelings
	of insignificance and inadequacy,
I will praise Your name and proclaim Your love
	to people all around me.

23

The Lord is my constant companion.
There is no need that He cannot fulfill.
Whether His course for me points
> to the mountaintops of glorious joy
> or to the valleys of human suffering,
> He is by my side.
> He is ever present with me.
He is close beside me
> when I tread the dark streets of danger,
> and even when I flirt with death itself,
> He will not leave me.
When the pain is severe,
> He is near to comfort.
When the burden is heavy,
> He is there to lean upon.
When depression darkens my soul,
> He touches me with eternal joy.
When I feel empty and alone,
> He fills the aching vacuum with His power.
My security is in His promise
> to be near me always
> and in the knowledge
> > that He will never let me go.

24

Let us never forget that this world
and everything in it belongs to God.
But not all of this world's citizens
recognize or give allegiance to their Creator.

Who are the ones who truly love and serve God?
They are the people who discover and live
within His purposes for their lives.
They are the people whose hearts and hands
are dedicated to His will for them.
They are the people who turn away from
self-centered concerns
to live for those around them.
They can count on God's perpetual blessings.
They have been delivered from anxiety
to focus their efforts on communicating
God's eternal love to people around them.

Let us look up and live!
God is present in all His glory and majesty.
Let us let go and celebrate!
Our loving Lord is here with us
and will manifest Himself through us.
We represent Him in all His saving power.
We are His beloved and empowered servants
in this world that He created.

25

I am reaching for You again, O God.
From the abyss of defeat,
  the suffocating shame of failure,
   I seek Your mercy and Your help.
Enable me to see Your will for my life.
Break through this stifling darkness
  with some direction, some meaning,
  some purpose for my existence.
You are my God; You have promised me salvation.
How long must I wait for Your response?

Have You given up on me, O Lord?
Are You remembering the uncountable times
  that I have failed You?
Then I am remembering Your steadfast love,
  Your concern for those
   who fail and fumble,
  Your efforts to restore those
   who humbly reach out for You.
I know well that those
  who walk in Your course for their lives
   find contentment and fulfillment.
I have tried to do so, and again I have failed.
I am aware that those who serve You
  will know true security and abundance.
I have sought this only to be snared
  and incapacitated by my own weaknesses.

O God, have mercy!
I know my guilt is great.
Look upon my emptiness and loneliness,
      consider kindly my afflictions and despair,
      remember the perpetual presence
          of my human weaknesses and instincts.
Regard once more the pernicious and violent forces
      that oppose Your will in my life.
Forgive me my many sins,
      and restore me to Yourself.
Watch over me and hold on to me, O God,
      lest I fall again.

26

I am about to make an important decision, Lord,
    and the day before me is charged with uncertainty.
Enable me to sense Your presence,
    to feel Your strengthening power,
    to be assured of Your guiding concern.

I have been Your child and servant for many years.
Even in my youth I claimed Your redeeming love
    and dedicated my life to Your purposes.
Until now I have shunned the world's enticements,
    the human ambitions that so teasingly beckon,
    to pursue Your objectives
        and carry out Your commands.

I have been faithful to the hour of worship
    and the time of prayer.
I have celebrated Your grace and sung Your praises.
My dearest friends are those who love and serve You.

Now, O Lord, I have come to a fork in the road.
I don't know which way to turn.
I commit this day into Your hands.
I pray that it may be lived by Your direction
    and in accord with Your will.

I raise my voice in thanksgiving, O God,
    for You have granted me the assurance
        that You will guide my faltering steps.

27

*W*ith the living and eternal God as my goal and guide,
  fear and anxiety need have no place in my life.
All the evil in the world cannot destroy Him
  nor can it destroy anyone within His loving embrace.
The very legions of hell lay siege to my soul,
  only to be thwarted by a power far greater.

I have one primary and ultimate desire:
  to abide within the love and acceptance of God.
Within His tender care I know I am safe.

Thus I shall stand tall
  regardless of threatening enemies
    and the tyranny of evil.
I will counter the subtle voices of temptation
  with exclamations of praise to my God.

My God does hear when I cry out to Him.
He does not ignore my needs;
  neither is He indifferent to my desires.
He will not let me go even if my own family
  should turn against me.
He will sustain me and keep me on course
  through the dangers and pitfalls of this life.

It is possible to know and experience God's love
  in this uncertain, tumultuous existence.
Take courage, step out in faith, scorn the consequences,
  and let God have His way with you.

28

O God, I am crying for help!
This is not a pious exclamation—
      I mean it! I'm desperate!
If You don't listen, I'll go down the drain!

Don't let me float downstream
      with those who ignore You.
I know they will go over the edge if they persist
      in their course of rebelliousness and indifference.
Reach out, O God,
      and snatch me from this overpowering current
          lest I perish with them.

I thank You, O God.
You have heard my agonizing cry.
I called for You, and You responded.
You are my Hope and my Salvation.
I will sing Your praises forever.

And thus the Lord is the Hope and Salvation
      of all who trust in Him.
Stay close to those who struggle, O God,
      never let them go.

We need to give credit to whom credit is due.
God is alive,
>   and He deserves our perpetual praises.
There is reason for rejoicing.
There is a God to worship and love.

The skies and the forests
>   manifest His beauty.
The sweep of the ocean
>   represents His power.
The gigantic bodies suspended in
>   our universe portray His majesty.
The wind and the rain,
>   the lightning and the thunder,
>   the creatures that inhabit the land,
>   the flowers that brighten our lives,
>   all this comes from the hand of God.
The glory is not ours but God's.

Even the achievements
>   of human hand, mind, and machine
>   come through the wisdom and power
>   of the eternal God.
The contributions of science;
>   the fields ripe for harvest;
>   the control of water, air, and space;
>   the establishment of our great institutions—
>   these also reflect the glory of God.

Let us give credit to whom credit is due.
Let us rejoice in the God who blesses us.
Let us seek His grace to serve Him
    by serving others with the abundance
      that He bestows upon us.

In a world where there are people
    who assume You no longer exist,
      I am compelled to proclaim Your praises, O God.
I cannot define or describe You,
    but I know from personal experience
      Your power and presence in my life.
There was a time when I screamed,
    "Good Lord, where are You?"
Then You touched my despairing soul with healing
    and delivered me from my private little hell.
Thus I shout Your praises, O my God,
    and exhort all who know You to do the same.
There are times when I feel Your anger,
    but even then I know
      Your concern and love for me remain eternal.
Then my nights of despair
    resolve into the dawn of new joy.

There was a time when I thought I was secure
    among my material accumulations.
However, they gathered like a cloud
      to blot out the face of God,
    and I was left empty and unfulfilled.

I finally came to my senses
    and returned to You, O God.
"Lord," I said, "my well-deserved damnation
    would also be a loss to You.

I cannot praise You from the pits of hell
    or proclaim Your loving-kindness
        from the grave of eternal death.
So have mercy, Lord,
    and help me out of this dark fog."

And You turned my griping into gratitude,
    my screams of despair into proclamations of joy.
Now I can explode with praises,
    and I will spend eternity in thanksgiving to You.

I am up a blind alley, Lord.
The props have been knocked out from beneath me.
I feel as if I'm grappling with the wind
> for some support or security.
I've been pulled up short, Lord.
Now I realize how much I need
> something or someone
> beyond and above myself
>> to give stability to my tenuous existence.
Maybe it was Your doing, Lord.
Maybe You are bringing me back to home port,
> correcting my focus
>> and reassessing my goals.

I return to You with empty hands, Lord.
You know well my sorry plight.
I did not find that secret treasure,
> that pearl of great price.
The bright lights that beckoned
> only led me astray.
I became entangled in the bonds of self-service.
Everything I touched turned to dust in my hands.

I despise myself today, Lord.
Even those I thought were my friends
> turn their faces from me.
There is no place to go, nothing to cling to.
I can only come back to You

and cast myself on Your loving mercy.
You are my God.
You never let me out of Your sight.
Even when I strike out on my own,
    You pursue me and hold on to me.

I've stopped running, Lord.
From this point on
    I will place my hours and days
        into Your loving hands.
I seek only Your guidance
    and the grace and strength
        to carry out Your purposes.
Restore me, O God,
    to Your program and design for my life.

Thank You for taking me back, Lord,
    for renewing my relationship with You.
I seek now to walk in Your course for me.
I shall abide forever in Your steadfast love.
I will proclaim Your praises
    and live out Your purposes.
Enable me to be faithful to You,
      whatever the consequences,
    and to celebrate Your love
      and to communicate it to everyone around me.

_32_

The person who knows the meaning of forgiveness,
who is no longer plagued by past failures,
who stands blameless and guilt-free before God,
that person is rich indeed.

Every time I attempt to handle my own guilt—
by ignoring it, rationalizing it,
or just running away from it—
some unseen power or pressure
from the depths of my being
squeezes my life dry, leaving me empty.

But when I face up to my failures and confess them,
when I open my guilt-ridden heart
to You, O God,
then I realize the blessed meaning
of forgiveness.

Thus everyone who claims faith in the loving God
needs to cling to His acceptance and concern.
Times of darkness will come.
Life's storms and tempests will continue to rage,
but the faithful shall not be destroyed.

You are, O God, a place of refuge.
You enable us to face our problems,
You keep us from being destroyed by them.
Even within the darkness surrounding me,

in the midst of life's turmoil,
        I can hear the voice of God:
"Even these things serve a purpose in your life.
Don't sell them short
        for they are steps along My path for you.
Stop being stubborn and stupid
        like some undiscerning jackass
                that has to be driven with sticks or whips."

The faithful and the faithless both suffer
        the uncertainties and insecurities of this life,
        but the children of God can depend always
                on the love of their Father.
It is for this reason that there is
        light even in the midst of darkness,
        incomprehensible joy in the midst of sorrow,
        and we can find a measure of happiness
                and well-being
                regardless of the circumstances that surround us.

33

God is here—let's celebrate!
With song and with dance,
     with stringed instruments and brass,
     with cymbals and drums,
     let us express exuberant joy in God's presence.
Let us celebrate with the old songs of praise.
Let us also create new songs
     that portray the eternal love of our God.

He did create this world.
He continues to permeate it with His love.
Even among its frustrated and unbelieving children,
     He constantly carries out His purposes.
His plans for His world and its inhabitants
     are not obliterated by the foolishness
          of men and women.
His truth is not blotted out by the lethargy or lies
     of His apathetic creatures.
He continues to reign and to reveal Himself to us.

And God continues to create and to renew
     the world around us.
He does this through those who are His own,
     who rely on His ever-present love.
He delivers His children from the fear of death
     and through them gives life to this world.
God's love is sure and everlasting.
Hearts open to His love are filled with joy.
They truly find cause for celebration.

34

I feel as if I could never cease praising God.
Come and rejoice with me over His goodness!

I reached for Him out of my inner conflicts,
    and He was there
        to give me strength and courage.
I wept in utter frustration over my troubles,
    and He was near to help and support me.

What He has done for me He can do for you.
Turn to Him; He will not turn away from you.
His loving presence
    encompasses those who yield to Him.
He is with them
    in the midst of their troubles and conflicts.
He meets their emptiness with His abundance
    and shores up their weakness
        through His divine power.

Listen to me; I know whereof I speak.
I have learned through experience
    that this is the way to happiness.
God is ever alert to the cries of His children;
    He feels and bears with them
        their pains and problems.
He is near to those who suffer
    and reaches out to help
        those who are battered down by despair.

Even the children of God experience affliction,
   but they have a loving Father
      who will keep them and watch over them.

The godless suffer in loneliness, without hope;
   the servants of God find meaning and purpose
      even in the midst of suffering and conflict.

35

It is not easy, Lord, to follow after You.
While You take the hard road
      with joyous leaps and bounds,
    I stumble over every stone
      and slip into every rut.
You calmly weather each storm
      and walk fearlessly through the night.
I am buffeted by the winds,
      and I falter in the darkness.

And You always have answers, Lord,
      for those who confront You.
My tongue is thick and clumsy.
I cannot articulate what I believe
      or what they need to hear.
You have the wisdom and the power
      to meet the needs of people around You.
But I am foolish and ineffective,
      and my sisters and brothers turn away
         from me in disgust.

I have really tried to relate to people around me,
      to reach out in love and concern.
I have shared their sorrows and their joys.
I have shelved my ambitions
      to respond to their needs.

But when I fail to produce what they want,

or when I am limited by my humanity
and incapacitated by my personal problems,
they will have nothing to do with me.
I feel as if I have been used only to be abused.
I am squeezed dry and then cast aside.

Yet I must continue to follow You, O Lord.
It is a hard path to walk,
and I will falter at times.
I long intensely for an occasional oasis
along this journey through wind and sand.
I need desperately Your touch of joy and enrichment
as I labor amid the blood and tears
of this distorted world.
I am empty, Lord,
enable me to sense Your fullness
and grant to me the grace and the courage
to be faithful as Your child and servant.

36

It amazes me how some people can be so self-centered,
      so indifferent and calloused
         to the desires and needs of others.
Not only do they neglect God;
      they are totally oblivious of Him
         and have no fear of Him.
And then they convince themselves that this is life,
      that the world spins around them
         and they must satiate their own desires
            regardless of the hurt it causes others.

And yet Your all-pervading love, O God,
      which extends far beyond
         the dimensions of our conscious lives,
      includes even these distorted people
         who spurn You in exchange for
            twisted, self-centered lives.

Your eternal love is beyond comprehension.
No wonder Your children constantly reach for it
      and find security within it.
Within that love, O Lord, You answer our needs
      and fulfill our desires.

Continue to pour out Your saving love
      upon those who follow You.
Do not allow the arrogance and infidelity of the godless
      to deter us from Your course for our lives.

It's high time we stop complaining
    about the corruption of our world
      or the lack of values in our society.
It seems like at the same time we complain,
    we eye with envy those ungodly characters
      who appear to have more fun
        or to be more successful than we are.

If we really trusted in God
      and were truly committed to His purposes,
      the world might be better off today.
God is in our world.
He is the source
    of our joy and well-being,
    the fulfillment of our hearts' desires.
God works through those who are dedicated
    to Him and His will
      to permeate this world's darkness
        with divine light.

Let's stay calm and try to be patient.
Stop worrying
    about the apparent hopelessness of it all.
We only contribute to this despair
    with our negativity and defeatism.
God has not taken a vacation; He is here.
He has His own way of dealing
    with corruption and greed,

disease and bigotry,
war and violence,
insecurity and fear.

The ultimate victory is God's.
Those who live within God's will
shall surely discover
that His purposes prevail,
that true joy and peace and security
come from Him.

Let us wait on God and seek daily to obey Him.
He is our salvation and our security,
and nothing in this world
can take that away from us.
Ask Him to calm our hostilities,
to overcome our anxieties,
and to help us walk in peace and love.

O God, how angry You must be with me!
I feel as if I were
pierced through with a red-hot iron,
stifled with the heavy hand of judgment.

I am falling apart.
I am sick to death with sin and failure,
broken and spent, wretched and miserable,
flat on my face in despair.

Even those I once called my friends
now keep their distance
while others actually gloat over my predicament.
But I am becoming numb
to their glances of suspicion or pity
and their self-righteous rebukes.
I have ceased trying to defend myself
or respond to their accusations.
I've had it; I am ready to throw in the towel.
I simply cannot take it any longer.

You are aware of my anguish, my God.
You feel my misery.
I know that I have grieved You,
and I am truly sorry for my sin.
Don't turn away from me, O God.
Don't leave me in this abominable mess.
Save me now, O God, lest I be damned forever.

39

I said to myself, "I'll watch it—
I'll grit my teeth and hold in my anger
at least as long as I am
among ungodly people."

And I honestly tried, but it was no use.
The pressures increased.
The more I stewed about it,
the more frustrated I became.

Finally I exploded:
"O God, demonstrate some concern for me.
Give me some reason for this endless conflict,
some objective for this fast-ebbing life of mine.
You made me what I am,
and the span of my existence
is but a speck of dust to You.
This is true about every human being.
A person is no more than a smidgen of moist air
or a shadow without lasting substance.
Men and women endure this temporal turmoil
for no reason whatsoever.
They agonize and toil
only to leave the fruits for someone else to enjoy.

"So I wonder what in the world it's all about.
I have no hope at all except in You.
I continue to lay claim

to Your forgiveness for my failures.
Keep me from being
    despised and abhorred
      by my fellow creatures.
Lift Your heavy hand from me;
    I am utterly weary of its oppressing weight.
When You punish people with judgment of their failures,
    You suck up like a tornado
      everything that is precious to them.
Surely they are no more than a passing cloud
    on the eternal horizon.

"Hear and decipher these confusing thoughts of mine.
    Lend Your ear to these agonizing cries.
      Do not turn away from my pains and problems.
I am just a swiftly passing traveler,
    as were all who have gone before me.
Let me have just a morsel of happiness
    before I leave this world
      and enter into oblivion."

40

I searched long and shouted loud for God.
It finally paid off. He responded.
He reached into my pathetic emptiness
    and planted objective and purpose.
Now I feel like singing;
    there is genuine meaning in my life.
And I can tell others about the
    prominent place God holds in my heart.
Those who are thoroughly fed up
      with the fly-by-night objectives
        of this ephemeral existence,
    who will look to their Creator
      and seek out His will for them,
    they also will find something to sing about.
There is love and concern in Him,
    and meaning and purpose,
      far more than one can possibly imagine.

Our God is not looking for genius;
    He does not require great talent.
He is not charmed by our panic-ridden activity.
He simply asks for our faith and our obedience.
It was when He turned me from self-seeking
    to follow His will for my life
      that I discovered serenity and security.

Thus I am compelled to express in word and in deed
    the glad news of God's love and concern

to anyone who will listen.
And the Lord knows
    that I have honestly tried to do this.
My frailties and my failures are many,
    but I have not cheated on this score.
I have proclaimed the salvation
    that God offers to all.

But my conflicts have not ceased.
My sin-permeated nature still plagues me.
I still feel overwhelmed at times
    by my faults and fallibilities.
I am disturbed and depressed
    when others fail to understand or accept me.
I need to rely on the grace of God.

God grant that all who search for life's meaning
        may discover it
            in a relationship of love and trust with Him.
Then they shall know His greatness
        and proclaim His praises.
As for me, foolish and sinful though I am,
        I know that God will never cease to love me.

41

I believe that people who give of themselves
    for the sake of others,
   who demonstrate genuine concern
    for those who are less fortunate,
   are especially blessed by God.
They are precious in God's eyes
   and are protected by Him.
Even as they face the hatred of their enemies
    or the conflicts and illnesses of this existence,
   the Lord delivers and sustains them.

It is for this reason that I dare to claim
   God's gracious intervention on my behalf.
It is true that my sins are many.
I reach desperately for God's forgiving mercy.
I receive no comfort from many
   who I thought were my friends.
I could drop dead; they couldn't care less.
When we meet,
   their words are empty,
   their thoughts pregnant with suspicion.
When we part,
   they go out to spread their suspicions abroad,
    imagining the worst about me
     and whispering behind my back.

I can imagine their conversation:
   "One would think she'd be

beyond this sort of thing.
Why she's as bad as the worst of them.
She's had it! She won't crawl out of this!"
Even the one person I trusted the most,
    in whom I confided,
  with whom I lovingly related,
  even she looks down her nose at me
    as one she would rather step on than support.
She no longer wants anything to do with me.

My loving God, You are truly gracious to me.
You have not cast me aside
  or allowed me to be destroyed.
You know that I honestly want to serve You.
And You have demonstrated
  Your acceptance and concern for me
    by sustaining me
    and drawing me even closer to Yourself.
May God be praised forever!

42

As a desert wanderer longs for springs of cool water,
      so my thirsty soul reaches out for You, O God.
How I long for a deeper sense of Your presence,
         for a faith that will embrace You
            without fear or doubt!
Yet while I weep in longing, people around me say,
         "If God is not dead, where is He?"

I remember so well the faith of my childhood.
How real God was to me in those days
         when I prayed and sang praises
            and listened to His Word
               in the fellowship of family and friends!

Then why am I so depressed now?
Why can't I recapture the joy and confidence
         of those years?
I remember the stories of Your love
         that I was taught;
How merciful and all-powerful were Your dealings
         with Your children throughout history!
Yet now my heart is empty,
         and waves of doubt flood over my soul.

I pray, but the heavens, too, are empty.
It is almost as if God has forgotten all about me.
And while I struggle with the sickness of doubt,
         people around me say,

"If God is not dead, where is He?"
O foolish heart, why do you seethe in unrest?
God has not changed;
   His love for me is ever the same.
He will renew my faith in Him;
   I can again shout His praises
      even when I don't feel His presence.
Truly He is God,
   and He is my Help and my Hope.

43

O God,
     my life is cluttered with conflicts.
And there are times
     when You seem oblivious to it all.
The pitfalls before me, the weaknesses within me—
     all this is most depressing.
I feel as if I am groping in utter darkness.

Break into my darkness, O God.
Set me free from my hang-ups.
May the daily pressures
          that threaten to strangle me
     drive me to Your fountainhead of grace.
Then night will give way to dawn,
          depression shall resolve into joy,
               and I shall sing Your praises once more.

O foolish spirit,
     why do you fret over so many things?
God is here!
He knows all about your troubles and trials.
Renew your faith in Him and rejoice.

I shall rejoice!
No matter how dark the night,
     God is my ever-present and eternal Hope.

44

$\mathcal{O}$ *God,*
     I have heard so much about how close You were
          to Your children throughout history.
They conquered the enemy
     and credited You for their victories.
When they were defeated,
     they accepted their lot
          as Your righteous judgment.
They assumed they were Your beloved charges
          and accepted their afflictions
          as from Your hand.
Their persistent faith in You
     held them together
          through the crises of their lives.

And I am aware of how You have watched over me
     in the midst of my conflicts.
You have enabled me to overcome
     the obstacles in my life.
Even when I failed miserably,
     You set me on my feet again
          and directed me on Your course for my life.
I am keenly aware of my incapabilities
     and inadequacies
          and of how much I need You.
I know all this, Lord.
You have been an integral part
     of my life's experiences.
I am deeply grateful for Your care and concern.

But what about today, O Lord?
I am on the spot—and I can't reach You.
It seems as if You have left the scene
     and I am left holding the bag.
I cry for help
     and hear only the echo of my own voice.
I grope around me
     and find insurmountable walls and dark corners.
The advice of my peers and superiors
     seems devoid of genuine love or concern.
O God, if You are truly my God,
     reveal Yourself to me now.
I simply cannot bear the shame and the pain
     of my problem.
Nobody around me can help me.
If people knew about it,
     they would only shun me.

I have not forgotten You, O God.
I do believe in You as I have been taught.
I worshiped You and sang Your praises
     when all was well.
I have dedicated my life to You and Your purposes.
Now I am in deep trouble.
I have no one else to turn to.

O God, listen to me.
Respond to my cry for help.

Deliver me from this terrible conflict
    before it destroys me.
Help me sense Your loving concern.
Save me before it is too late.

45

My heart is full of joy today.
I reach almost frantically for the sounds
      that might express that joy,
         the words that would proclaim the exuberance
         that I feel at this moment.
I am overwhelmed with praise,
      and I must express it lest I succumb to it.

You, my dear friend, were the source of this joy.
You touched me with love
      and awakened my sleeping heart
         to the beauty and fragrance of life around me.
God reached out through your devotion and concern
      to kindle anew a fire within me,
         to fan embers into flames of light and faith.
You marched into my jungle of despair
      and made a path for me to walk on once more.
You sliced through my confusion
      and gave order and motivation
         to my purposeless gropings.

I am so very grateful—to God and to you.
I pray that God may use me,
      as He has so abundantly used you,
      to transmit joy to the joyless,
         despairing lives of those who cross my path.
And I pray that God may bless you
      and keep you and use you forever.

Our great God is still our Refuge and Strength.
He knows our problems and fears.
Thus we have no business doubting Him
　　even though the earth is convulsed in tragedy
　　　　or its human masses threatened
　　　　　　by ethnic hatred, disease,
　　　　　　drugs, crime, or abuse.

God continues to reign as all-wise
　　and as almighty as ever.
His eternal plan is not canceled out
　　by the whims of human leaders
　　　　or the freakish accidents of nature.
Nations will destroy each other.
　　Civilizations will perish.
　　The earth itself may one day become
　　　　a smoking cinder, but God will not leave us.
He is forever our sure Refuge and Strength.

Just look around you; read the pages of history.
Refresh your flagging spirit with the reminder
　　of His great feats throughout the ages.
And you will again hear Him speaking:
　　"Relax, stop fretting, and
　　　　remember that I am still your God.
　　I still hold the reins of this world."

God is here among us.
　　He continues to be our Refuge and Strength.

47

Clap your hands! Stomp your feet!
Let your bodies and your voices
    explode with joy.
God is not some human concoction.
He is for real! And He is here!
Despite all attempts
        to rationalize Him out of existence,
    God is in our world,
        and He reigns over our universe.

The rulers of nations often ignore Him.
People of learning often pass Him by.
The masses of His creatures substitute
    their own little gods in His place
    and worship the things they can see and feel.
Others build fortresses around themselves
    and announce no need for God.

Our great God will not be ignored.
He will not remove Himself from our world.
Let us recognize His presence
    and fill the air with His praises.

48

How great is my God!
He soars above our poor intellects
    like a snow-capped mountain
        over a sun-baked desert.
He scatters the profound theories
        of wise men and women
    like leaves pushed around by a winter wind.
He shatters
    the assembled might of world governments
        as an earthquake levels a city.
He reaches down in tenderness
        to earth's poor creatures
    and draws them to Himself.

Consider with me the greatness of my God.
Measure His judgments;
    embrace His eternal love.
Stand tall in your faith,
        courageous in your commitment,
    for He is truly a great God.

49

How foolish are the creatures of God!
They accumulate wealth
    and imagine themselves secure
        in possessions and property.
Or they use some inborn gift
    and bask in the plaudits of their peers.
They live for themselves alone
    and give no thought to eternity.
They claim that God is simply
    not necessary to their existence.
He is just a big thumb in the sky
    designed to pacify the weak and the childish.
They claim that they must be
    sufficient unto themselves.
They don't need the extra baggage
        of faith and religion.

But when riches melt away,
    health fails, talents wear thin,
    and remaining years become few,
    when no one honors them
        or expresses concern,
Then these foolish creatures stand naked and exposed
        in empty despair.
Their fortress is breached;
    they are flattened and defeated.
Life, what little of it there is left,
    no longer has meaning for them.

Then they may look desperately for the God
  they discarded in their youth.

Let us consider carefully the security
  of a loving relationship with God.
Let us mouth His praises
    and demonstrate in our lives the eternal joy
      of knowing Him and living as His children.
We need not depend on this world's wealth
    nor the accolades of human beings.
We need not fear the end of our days
    upon this earth.
God is forever—
    and also the souls of those
      who are committed to Him.

Clap your hands! Shout for joy!
God is real, and He is here!

50

God is indeed in our world.
From dawn to dusk,
from twilight hours to the first light
on the eastern horizon,
God is near us and around us.

God speaks to our world.
He speaks gently in love
and thunders fiercely in judgment.
He calls to those who are faithful to Him.
He comforts them and challenges them.
He secures them and sends them forth.

God is at work in our world.
He works in and through the lives of His children
who are loyal and obedient to Him.
"Don't bring your sacrifices to human altars
or build churches and erect memorials
on My behalf,"
He would say to us today.
"I already own the gifts you bring.
All these things have come to you from My hand.
You are to offer them on the altar of humanity's need.
These are the sacrifices that get through to Me
and are accepted by Me."

It is thus that God touches the lives of needy people.
It is by way of the self-sacrificing love
of His servants.

God judges our world.
This judgment falls upon those
who live totally for themselves.
They are indifferent to the needs of others.
No matter how impressive their rituals
and religious exercises,
their lives do not please God.

God is in our world.
We serve Him with the kind of worship
and thanksgiving
that effectively communicates His love
to His children in need around us.

51

O God, may the measure of Your eternal love
  be the measure of Your mercy.
And may the measure of Your mercy
    be sufficient to blot out my great sins
      and cancel out the guilt of my wrongdoings.

I have failed, O Lord, and my failures
    weigh heavily upon my heart.
I cannot share them all with my brothers or sisters
    lest they weigh too heavily upon them
      or even threaten our relationship.
But You know what they are, O God,
    and how far I have fallen short
      of Your standards and expectations.

I am only human, Lord.
It was not by my choice that I was propelled
    into this fractured world.
The weaknesses that plague me
      are not all my doing
      nor can I handle them by my strength alone.

I know that nothing can be hidden from You.
I can only acknowledge my indictment
    and beg for Your loving forgiveness.
Purge me of my guilt, O Lord.
      Heal the hurts of those
        who have been afflicted by my failures.

Revive my flagging spirit, O God.
Restore to me the joy and assurance
of a right relationship with You.
Reinstate me in Your purposes,
and help me avoid
the snares and pitfalls along this earthly path.

It is only then that my tongue will be set free
to sing Your praises
and my hands to perform the tasks
You have set before me.
It is only then that I can have a
deep and meaningful relationship
with my brothers and sisters,
and communicate to them
the message of Your reconciling love.

I bring You no oblation or sacrifice, my God,
only a foolish and self-centered heart.
I come to You with a sincere desire
to be Your servant,
to walk in Your course for my life,
to bask in Your love and reflect it
to those around me.

I thank You, God, that this is acceptable to You
and that I will remain Your child forever.

52

There are many clever people
    who apparently have no need for God.
With their keen wits and sharp tongues,
      they seduce their fellow creatures and use them
        to promote their own selfish ambitions.
They barge around this world as if they owned it
    and have no consideration for those
      they hurt in the process.
They brashly step on one another
    in their avid pursuit of riches and power.
They scorn those they brush aside
    and destroy those who stand in their way.
They flaunt their achievements before others
    and brag about their self-sufficiency.
They demean those poor fools
    who support and applaud them
      in their ascent to their worldly thrones.

They will be toppled,
    these ambitious people and their thrones of clay.
From the dust they came;
    to the dust they shall return.
Their cleverness will dissolve into emptiness.
Their boasting will become like a hot wind.
Their achievements shall become as nothing,
    and they shall grovel before the victims
      of their atrocious acts.

This is not so with the children of God.
They may never know earthly success
   and may never be inundated with temporal riches,
   but they are eternally secure in the love of God.
Like green trees that spread their boughs
      to shield the weary traveler
   or hold out their fruit to the hungry stranger,
   God's children quietly and continually carry out
      God's purposes in a barren land.

53

Those who proclaim that God is dead
    are veritable fools.
They presume to speak
        as sophisticated intellectuals;
        they are in reality, possibly unconsciously,
            promoting depravity.

God is ever probing the hearts of men and women,
    marking those who seek after Him.

He finds instead
        that great masses of His creatures
            are following after other gods.
And without realizing it,
        they are leading one another
            to certain destruction.
It is no wonder there is such confusion and terror
        in the world.
It is mostly perpetuated
        by those who have no use for God.
O may our great God restore
        the hearts of His foolish creatures
            to Himself.

54

I come in thanksgiving and praise, O God.
Help me articulate the gratitude
    that I feel toward You.

I was tripped up by my own pride
    and confounded by my own foolishness.
I said things and did things that hurt others
    and dishonored You.
I stumbled into a net of my own making
    from which I could not escape.

Then You heard my cries and saw my plight.
You touched me with Your love and set me free
    to walk with You once more.
You continue to deliver me
    from the snares and pitfalls surrounding me.

This is why I rejoice, O God.
It is because of this that I offer myself to You.
May Your ever-present love for me
    urge me to demonstrate love toward others
        who are troubled and afraid.

55

I am terribly alone, O God,
    and I don't know where to turn.
I thought I was really living
    when I came to the city—
        set free from the restraints
            of childhood and youth.
But now I am frightened.
The people around me are cold and indifferent.
No one knows that I exist.
The traffic by day and the neon glare
        that pushes back the night
        are strange and unfriendly.
I feel as if I am hopelessly lost
    in some concrete wilderness.
The streets lead nowhere—
    except to blend into other streets.
It's a wilderness filled with violence.
Its creatures are dazed, sick, hungry, or angry.
Oppression, crime, and injustice flourish.
Blood often flows in the streets.
And I can hardly see the blue sky by day
        or the stars by night
    or hear the songs of birds
        or the tolling bells of a church.

It was exciting at first.
I even had a friend with whom I explored
    the mysteries of the city.

Maybe I could have endured
    and found happiness with my friend.
But my friend turned into an enemy
    who no longer needed me
    and melted into the crowds
      that walk down my street.

Then the city became barren and desolate.
The bright lights became ghostly,
    the people around me like zombies
      or puppets on strings,
    the clamor and noise hideous and discordant.
And now my soul has become as bleak
    as the city.

I am lonely, O God, but I am not alone.
You are here in the city.
O God, lead me to You.
Enable me, my God,
    to serve You here in the city.

_56_

O God, I have tried diligently
to reflect Your love to people around me.
I shared my possessions;
I gave of my time;
I used Your gifts to me to support,
to help, and to bless others
who were in need.

But I feel as if I have been used, O God.
People have wiped their feet on me.
They take what I offer and then go their own way,
totally oblivious to my problems and pains.
They act as if I were in debt to them—
as if it were my duty to share myself with them.

But even as I groan in complaint, O Lord,
I know that this is Your course for me.
Even as they use You, so they will use me.
Truly, O God, I have nothing to lose,
for it is in losing that I truly find
that which is of everlasting value.

You are aware of my frustrations,
my feelings of emptiness and loneliness.
You have promised to replenish me
and use me to channel Your eternal springs
to those suffering around me.

I am emptied again and again—
    only to be filled from Your boundless resources.
Through me Your blessings are poured out
    upon those in need.

You have delivered me from the wasteland.
Therefore I dedicate myself anew
    to the task of sharing Your gifts
        with those still treading a parched path.

57

Encompass me with Your love and mercy,
    gracious Lord;
        I have no security except in You.
I am continually exposed
    to the destructive forces of this existence.
I am in constant danger of losing the battle
    to the passions and desires
        of my own nature.
I can only submit myself to You
    and trust that You will fulfill
        Your purposes in me.

Your love, O God, is steadfast;
    Your grace is everlasting.

Even when I am beaten down by depression,
    ensnared by my weaknesses and frailties,
    and even when my own lust threatens to devour me,
        You are my God,
            and You will not let me go.

I am determined to serve You, O Lord.
May my life be a continual thankoffering to You.
I shall sing Your praises forever.

*M*y *heart grieves, O Lord,*
    for the leaders of this world
        who play god with the lives of men and women.
With the clever twisting of half-truths
    they gather followers into their folds
        and manipulate them
        into carrying out their purposes.
They blind people to personal conscience
        and responsibility
    and enslave them to their immoral wishes
        and sinful ambitions.

Then there are velvet-voiced mystics who assume
        they are God's special gift to humankind
    and who,
        through devious tricks or inscrutable gifts,
        create their cults of loyal disciples.

You shall have the last word, O God,
    and those who take Your place,
        or who stand in Your way
        as You seek to draw people to Yourself,
    will be subjected to Your judgments.

You are my God, Almighty and Eternal.
Forbid, O God, that I should ever turn from You
    to follow the false shepherds of this world.

59

Deliver me, O God, from the enemies of my soul.
I am no longer afraid of people who stand in my way,
     even those who obstruct Your purposes
          or who deceive their fellow beings
          with their arrogant and clever clichés.
They anger me, but they do not frighten me.
My pain and confusion come because
     of my own weaknesses and faithlessness.

I strive for success and am fractured by failure.
I reach for eternal joy
     and am clobbered with depression.
I wait for guidance,
     and Your heavens are gray with silence.
I ask for Your Spirit
     and am confronted with emptiness.
I seek opportunities
     and run into stone walls.

I overcome these pernicious demons
          in the morning
     only to face them again
          when day turns into night.
They refuse to die, these persistent devils.
They plague my days and haunt my nights
     and rob me of the peace and joy
          of God-motivated living.
And yet, O Lord, You have surrounded my life

like a great fortress.
There is nothing that can touch me
    save by Your loving permission.
My faith will falter at times,
    but You will never fail me.

Teach me, O God,
    to live by Your Word and promises,
    to sing Your praises,
    to carry on within Your purposes
    despite these taunting, tempting enemies
      of my soul.

60

You made us, O God, a great nation.
The lands beyond our own
tremble at our awesome might.
But the rich wine of material wealth dulled our senses.
The tyranny of things obscured our vision.
We grew arrogant, self-satisfied,
and were often insensitive to the needs
of Your creatures beyond our borders.

We waved our swords menacingly
at potential enemies of our great country.
We established our outposts
in the very heart of our enemies' camps.
We extended our powerful tentacles
into other nations' undeveloped resources
and drew their blood into our own.
And we did this in Your name,
and we convinced ourselves
that it was by Your will.

Now our defenses have been broken, O Lord.
Our fortress has been breached.
We have given birth to offspring
that threaten us from within.
Splinter groups within our boundaries
assert their identity and threaten to destroy
our trust in unity under the flag.
Disillusioned youth rebel against

a seemingly hopeless future and create
    fear through might of ill-gotten and ill-used arms.
Buildings explode, innocent lives are taken,
    young blood is spilled over turf conflicts.
And as if the violence in the streets weren't enough,
    our religious institutions are under bombardment
        from New Age philosophies that
        subtly soften and erode our faith
        in the one true God.
We are becoming paralyzed by fear
    and polarized by the extreme actions
        of radical and reactionary people.

Your Word is clear
    for those who would follow You, O God.
Your promises are assured
    for the nation that will worship You.
The enemies that threaten us
    and the problems that beset us
    can be absolved only when we return to our God.
        He will guide us
        and make us a blessing to the world.

We seek Your help, O Lord,
    in restoring our great nation.

_61_

Listen to me, O God,
  listen to what I have to say.
From the bowels of this fractured world,
  I cry out my fears and longings.

I cannot find peace or security
    until I lose myself in something or someone
      that is greater than I.
Draw me more deeply into Your life and purposes;
    only then will I find shelter from the tempests
      of this fearful and uncertain existence.

You know that I am committed to You.
And because I am committed,
    I have inherited the same divine promises
      that are given to all who follow You.
Grant me the grace
    to fulfill my pledge of loyalty and service,
    and I shall never cease to sing Your praises.

As for me, my heart waits on God.
I know that my salvation comes from Him.
I may change my views about many things,
    but as for my need for God and His love,
        that is one conviction
        that shall never change.

There are many who would like
    to sabotage a person's deepest convictions.
With the skillful use of words and logic,
    they try to destroy
        the very foundations of faith.
As for me, my heart waits on God.
He is my Hope and my Help.
The temporal values that people focus on
    are so quickly lost
        amid the tempests of this life.
Their highest aspirations
    burst forth like bright flares
        only to fizzle out like wet fuses.

But my God offers a security that is eternal.
It cannot be logically defined,
    but it can be experienced.
Commit your life to Him,
    and you shall discover an anchor that will hold firm
        despite the chaos of this existence
        or the prattle of defiant unbelievers.

63

Like a thirsty child reaching for a drink,
   I grasp for You, O God.
And I have found You.
I have sensed Your holy presence
      in the worship service;
      in the hour of prayer,
         I have felt You to be near.
I realize now that Your love for me
      is far better than life itself.

My heart is full of joy and contentment.
My mouth is filled with praises for You.
Even the night hours are no longer lonely
      as I contemplate Your tender concern for me.

The enemies of my soul still seek to betray me,
      but they shall not snatch me out of Your hand.
And now that I have found You,
      I shall be secure and happy forever.

Listen to me, O God,
 I think I have good reason to complain.

I try very hard to follow Your paths
 and to serve Your purposes.
But I am deeply disturbed
 about the enemies and pitfalls
 that I unsuspectingly meet
 around every corner.
I find them in the tumultuous passions
 of my own being.
Much as I seek
 to rid myself of these overwhelming forces,
 they continue to clutch at my soul
 and to trip me up as I strive to please You.
I become so tired of this perpetual conflict
 with my sin-permeated nature.

And then I run into opposition
 in the reactions of trusted friends.
Their suspicions and unjust criticisms
 leave me withered and dried up
 in depression and discouragement.

Now it is the cunning words of the worldly-wise
 and the intellectual giants of this age
 that threaten the very foundations
 of what I so intensely believe.

Renew my faith, O Lord, and strengthen my belief
    that those who foolishly oppose You
        will fail in their attempts
            to thwart Your purposes.
Hold before me Your promise: Those who trust in You
    are truly and eternally secure,
        even amid continuous conflict and antagonism.

You well-deserve the praises of *Your children, O God,*
and they should fulfill their pledges to You.

Everyone must eventually face up to You,
and it must be with all
our sins and shortcomings.
But those who come in sorrow and repentance
shall find You merciful and gracious.
You, O Lord, shall forgive their sins
and fill their hearts with Your love and joy.

O God, You reach out to save us.
You are the single, eternal Hope of all humankind.

You make Your power known to us
in the majestic grandeur of the mountains,
in the thunderous roar of ocean waves.
Your abundance is poured out upon us
in the grain-laden fields,
in the flocks and herds in the meadows,
in the gentle rain that caresses the green hills.
Your love for us is manifested
in Your great acts of deliverance on our behalf.

You well-deserve the praises of Your children, O God.

66

It is high time we start making
    happy noises about God,
    that we boldly proclaim His name
      and shout His praises.

We already know
    what He has done throughout history,
      the great deeds He has performed,
      the people who witnessed them
        and worshiped Him.
Let us recognize, as well,
    what He is constantly doing for us.

He walks with us into the crucible of conflict.
    He tests and tries us
      in the valley of pain and sorrow.
    He allows us to taste the agony of affliction.
    He gives our enemies permission
      to oppose and oppress us.
And then He uses these very things
    to purge and prepare us for His purposes.

Now I renew my pledge to my God.
I strive to carry out those promises I made to Him
    when I cried for His help in my troubles.
I yield my life to Him
    as a sacrifice and thankoffering.

You who are seeking God,
    these are the things He has done for me:
He has accepted me despite my sins and failures.
He listens when I cry to Him,
    and He responds with solace and support.

I proclaim God's praises
    because I know He will love me forever.

67

May we continually be
    the recipients of God's mercy and blessing
so we may demonstrate
    His order and purpose throughout the earth
    and His redemptive power
        to the creatures of this world.

And may it ultimately result
    in all of God's sons and daughters
        lifting their voices in
            praise to their Lord and God.

The nations of the earth would truly
        abide in peace and sing for joy
    if God were to be their God
    and if they would direct their actions
        according to His will.
Then the inhabitants of this world would surely
    lift their voices in praise to their Lord and God.

The earth continues to receive
    the abundance of God.
His blessings are all around us.
May every mountain and valley, plain and forest,
        every city and every sprawling suburb
            echo with the praises of men and women
                to their God.

*W*e long for the day when *God* will take over our land,
    when wickedness will be suppressed
        and selfishness subdued,
    when people will begin to care for one another.

There will be clean air to breathe
    and pure water to drink.
There will be better schools for the young,
    hospitals for all who are ill,
    and jobs for those who seek them.
Everyone will feel needed and loved—
    the child, the laborer,
    the executive, the senior citizen.
There will be dignity and freedom and equal rights,
    no matter our ethnic or economic background.
There will be homes to live in
    and parks to play in.
There will be libraries and theaters
    and halls of learning.
There will be a place for everyone to live
    and work and learn and rest and play.
And people will have time for one another.

O how we will praise God in such a land!
Our voices will join in a great chorus of celebration.
Daily we will offer thanksgiving to our God,
    who rules over our land.
And everyone will have time for one another.

But God does not rule over our land.
Our streets are pregnant with crime.
The poor and dispossessed gather at
        shelters and food banks.
Our schools are overcrowded and inadequate.
We choke on the air we breathe.
We stumble over our own litter and waste.
We neglect the old and ignore the young.
We rush pell-mell from appointment to appointment.
And no one cares for one another.

You seek, O God, to rule over our land.
You have given us pure air and green hills
        and great forests and clean rivers.
You have showered us with Your abundant gifts—
        all that we need to make our land splendid.
And You have given us Your love
        and the command to care for one another.

We have failed You, O God.
        We have sucked to our individual bosoms
                the gifts of Your love,
        but we have never really learned
                how to care for one another.

You have rebuked us for our selfishness, O Lord.
We are smothering in the waste
        of our self-centered living.

Deliver us, O God,
>restore to us a land worthy of Your habitation,
>and teach us, O loving God,
>>how to care for one another.

69

O God, at this time I find myself
backed up against the wall,
at the bottom of the barrel,
at the end of my rope.
There is no place to go but up.
Save me, O God, before it is too late.

I can't even cry out any longer;
I can't even pray, so deep is my despair.

O Lord, You know the ugliness of my failure.
How sorely it must grieve You!
Forbid that others may be hurt by my foolishness
or that my errors and faults might lead them astray.
I have been trying to represent You to them;
instead I have brought dishonor and disrespect
to my witness and Your name.
Now even those who once loved me
keep their distance;
those who listened in respect
turn away in disgust.

Maybe my intense
eagerness to carry out Your purposes
has become my stumbling block,
and now I am being ridiculed for my zeal.
They make fun of me;
they whisper about me behind my back.
O God, don't let me go down the drain.

Respond, in Your great love,
    to my unhappy plight.
Raise me from the mire of despair,
    the darkness of depression.
Deliver me from these human weaknesses
    that plague me and lead me into defeat.
You know what they are, O Lord,
    and You know the limits of my endurance.
You know, as well, the pain of my failure
    and the abject loneliness I feel
      when I lose the battle.

You know, O God,
    and You reach forth in mercy
      to rescue and deliver.
You sometimes permit failure
      and defeat in my life
    so my relationship with you
      can be revived and renewed.
Thus I again will sing the praises of God
    and make thankofferings to Him.

May all those who are
      beaten down by failure and despair
    see anew Your love
    and experience Your deliverance
    and be restored once more
      to joy and purposefulness.

70

O God, may You take pleasure in setting me free
and in securing me
from the enemies of my soul.
Keep them from bringing
shame upon Your servant
and dishonor to Your name.

May those who sincerely seek You
find genuine happiness and fulfillment,
and may they express their joy
in proclamations of praise to You.
As for me, I always
need Your sustaining grace.
O God, do not withhold it from me.

Good Lord, You have kept me
within the secure embrace of Your love
these many years.
My life is one long list of divine deliverances.
I have come running to You again and again
when the forces of evil
set themselves against me.

From the moment of my birth,
I was dedicated to Your will,
given life by You
only to yield it back to You.
And since that time, the days and hours of my life
have been filled with praise for You.

But the enemies that plagued me in my youth
still lay siege to my soul,
looking for chinks in my armor,
for loopholes in my defenses,
through which to enter and lay waste.

Now, as I near
the late afternoon and evening of my life,
I continue to seek Your love and mercy.
Even while I shout Your praises
and proclaim Your salvation,
I reach for the assurance
of Your love and concern.

You have guided me
    through my precarious youth,
    now I need Your grace for my senior years.
Fill my heart with purpose
    and my mouth with praises
    so I may continue to proclaim
        Your name and Your salvation
        to all who will listen.

You are, O God, the Creator and Performer
    of great and glorious things.
There is no one like You.
You have kept me safe throughout life's conflicts,
    led me through its crucible of experiences,
    drawn me back from its pitfalls and precipices,
    healed all my wounds,
        and comforted me in my afflictions.
Thus I know that You
    will continue to love and care for me.

I will dedicate my remaining days
    to praising You,
        espousing Your faithfulness,
        and proclaiming Your love and concern
            for all who will turn to You.
May every fiber of my being and
    every activity of my life
        resound with praises to my God.

_O_ _God of love,_
    grant to Your children the grace
        to represent You effectively
        in our discordant world.
Give us the courage
        to put our lives on the line
    to communicate life and truth
        to all Your creatures,
            wherever they may be found.

Where there is injustice,
        may we diagnose its cause
        and discover its cure.
Where there is bigotry,
        teach us how to love
        and how to encourage others to love.
Where there is poverty,
        help us share the wealth
        that has come from Your hand.
Where there is war and violence,
        make us peacemakers that lead
        men and women to Your eternal peace.

Help us, O God, to become what You
        have appointed and empowered us to become.
Where there is darkness,
        may we become the rays of Your sun
        that banish the gloom from lonely lives.
Where there is drought,
        let us be like gentle showers

that turn barren deserts into green meadows.
Where there is ugliness and distortion,
    enable us to portray the beauty and order
        of Your will and purposes.

Great God, You are in our world.
Your majesty is reflected
    in Your creation around us.
But there are multitudes who do not
    feel Your concern
        or acknowledge Your love.
Is it because Your servants have failed
        to carry out Your command and commission?
    or that we have yet to sense
        the significance of our salvation
        and the purpose of our mission?

Forbid, O God,
    that we be deaf to the cries of the poor
        or indifferent to those who have needs.
May we identify with those who are oppressed
    and help bear the burdens
        of those who suffer.
May we hear Your voice of concern
    and feel Your loving touch
        and as Your servants in this world,
            manifest You to people around us.
The glory is Yours, O God,
    and we shall praise Your name
        and celebrate Your cause together.

73

It is generally expected
that God will stand by the righteous
and remain close to those whose thoughts and deeds
are purely altruistic.
I am afraid I just don't belong
to that class of people.
I guess I am just a perpetual backslider.
Rather than thinking unselfishly,
I find myself envious and covetous
of those who have so much more than I do.

They never seem to have problems.
They are always so strong and healthy.
I doubt that they know the meaning of conflict.
They are proud, carefree,
and so disgustingly smug about everything.
They act as if God didn't even exist,
and they are almost blasphemous
in their attitudes and actions.

And yet people honor and applaud them;
they find nothing to censor about them.
What aggravates me is the obvious unconcern
about God or others.
Yet they always appear to be
so comfortable and well-off.

And all the while I struggle so desperately

with my sin-permeated nature.
I try so hard to please God,
>> yet my days are full of conflict,
>>> and my heart seethes in unrest.

I know I speak foolishly and unfairly,
>> but I get so fed up with it all.
That is, until I begin arguing with God about it.
Then I realize that those who are materially rich are
>> not as well-off as they appear.
Their bright bubble will burst some day;
>> their dream will turn into a nightmare.

It's just that I get so depressed at times,
>> and I act like a stupid fool.
It amazes me that even while engrossed
>>> in irrational and unspiritual contemplations,
>> I am never far from You, O Lord.
You hold me close to Yourself.
You guide me and watch over me.
You assure me that it is all worth it.
And because of this glorious truth,
>> I have no need for anything else.
The essential desires of my being are met in You, O God.
I shall be victimized often by human failure,
>> but my great God never ceases
>>> to love me and bless me.

How good it is to know that God is always near!

74

It disturbs and discourages me, O God,
to witness the apparent successes
of those who oppose You.
While Your children wrestle
with doubts and conflicts,
the agnostics and false religious leaders of our world
tear down the pillars of our faith
and gloat over our frustration.

They make fun of our rituals and symbols.
They dissect our dogmas
and ridicule our institutions.
They create godless philosophies
that seduce the young and confuse the old.

They deliberately obstruct our efforts
to represent You in our world.
As a result of their diabolical activities,
many have turned away from the true God
to worship lesser gods
and to chase after lesser goals.

We know, O God, how You have handled
Your enemies in the past.
We know that You cannot be dethroned,
that You are God over all creation.
Then how can You allow these God-defiers
to get by with what they are doing?

Consider our restlessness, O God.
Do not let them step on us and grind us under their feet.
Help us, O God,
     ineffective and foolish as we may be,
   to stand up to the demigods
     that plague our land.

*W*e *praise You, O God.*
Even in the midst of this world's wickedness,
    we celebrate Your majesty and power.

For You are here, O God.
You are here to save;
    You are here also to judge.
Even while the godless trumpet their rebellion,
    You hold the world in the palm of Your hand.
Should You close Your hand in anger, O God,
        their doom is sealed,
        their boasts ended forever.

Your fainthearted servants
    need not be dismayed, O God.
Even the rebelliousness of these obstinate creatures
    can serve to further Your purposes.
We need not fear the distortions
    of those who defy and oppose You.
We need only renew our relationship with You,
        rededicate our lives to Your objectives,
        and continue to celebrate Your presence
            and Your power in our world.

77

I cry to God in my desperation.
Out of the dark corner of my stifling loneliness,
    I grope in vain for some solace or comfort.

I try to think about God,
    to contemplate His many promises,
        but my heart is empty,
        my soul as dry as dust.
I spend sleepless nights searching,
    waiting for God to speak to my need,
        to give me strength in my conflict.
I remember how He has responded
    to my prayers in times past,
        but I get nothing from Him now—
            nothing except the echoes of my own agonized
                screams to the empty heavens.

I am reminded of His deeds
    and wonders of years past,
    how He demonstrated His love
        and concern for His people.
His majesty and power are reflected
    in the great forces of nature.
Then why doesn't He hear my pitiful pleadings?
Why doesn't He fulfill His promises to me?
Good Lord, where are You?

It would be good for us to consider God's dealings
with people and nations throughout history.
We ought to know these things;
    we have heard them again and again.
But we forget so quickly,
    and we fall so foolishly into the same pitfalls
        of infidelity and purposelessness.

God reached down and gathered a people for Himself.
He drew them into His fortress of love.
He revealed Himself to them
    through His commandments,
        which taught them how to live together in peace.
He enabled them to sense His presence
    in miraculous ways.
He poured out on them
    all that was needed to sustain them.
Even in the barren desert,
    food was rained on them from heaven,
    and water burst forth
        from the rocks around them.
He sent prophets to teach them
    and warriors to guide them
        through enemy country.
Like a shepherd who watches over his flock,
    our Lord watched over His children.

But like silly, confused sheep,

the children of God went astray.
They became self-sufficient and wandered off
    to pursue their own selfish interests.
Many of them rebelled against their God.
They refused His love and would not
    walk in His paths.

They became lost in the desert.
They suffered sorely for their sins.
They knew hunger and thirst and fear.
Only then did they remember
    the Creator of their youth
    and the loving care their heavenly Father provided
        when they walked in His paths.

Some of them turned back to God.
They discovered once more their loving God,
    a God willing to forgive them and accept them,
        to gather them once more
        into His fortress of love—
    to care for them and watch over them
        like a shepherd over his flock.

Like silly, selfish sheep,
    we often wander off on our own,
        imagining that we can find
        our own way to joy and security.

We discover pain and emptiness and meaninglessness
  outside the orbit of God.
We are out of joint,
    and the deepest longings of our hearts
      go unfulfilled.

I return, O God, to You
    and Your purposes for my life.
I find You waiting for me,
    ready to forgive my foolishness
    and my rebelliousness and eager
      to reinstate me in Your family
      and reconcile me to Your will once more.

I thank You, O God,
    for drawing me back to Your loving heart.

79

Why is it, O Lord,
   that the ungodly appear to be so successful?
They have no use for the church.
They play fast and loose with the lives of others.
They live solely for themselves
      and have no concern for individuals
         except to use them
            to further their personal ambitions.
They not only obstruct Your purposes, God,
      they pollute Your world and taunt Your servants.

Why do You let them do it, O Lord?
Why don't You seek satisfaction from Your enemies?
Why don't You show them,
         through Your faithful servants,
      that success comes to those
         who love and follow You?
      that we are on the right course?

Help me, O God, to love Your enemies
         even as You love them,
      to bear patiently and graciously their scorn,
      and to serve You faithfully
         whatever the consequences.
Help me measure my worth and success
         by Your standards
      and rejoice in Your love and acceptance.

O God, You are the Creator
and the Sustainer of Your church.
You have protected and prospered
Your faithful followers
throughout the stormy and tumultuous past.

Today we are in trouble.
Listen to our cries of consternation, O God.
We are confused and confounded.
We don't know where to turn,
in what direction to go.

We have prayed, O God.
We have sung Your praises.
We have proclaimed Your love to the world.
But today our power is slipping away,
our prestige is wearing thin.
People seem to have little respect for us anymore.
Those who have been brought up
within our structures
and have embraced our doctrines
are leaving the fold.
They say we no longer meet their needs
or the needs of the world.

You were with us in the beginning, Lord.
You planted us in the midst
of this world's turmoil.
You nurtured us and watched over us.
Despite the enemies

who sought to destroy us,
we grew until we encircled the earth.
Great halls of worship were built in Your honor, Lord.
Magnificent institutions were established
to carry out Your purposes.
Men and women dedicated their lives
to proclaim Your teachings.
Multitudes gathered to declare Your praises.

Today we are in trouble, Lord.
The walls are crumbling.
Our sanctuaries no longer attract the masses.
People dedicate their lives to other purposes.
We no longer make much of an impression
on this world of ours.

Renew Your church, O God.
We know You will never turn away
those who come to You
and will forever sustain
those who trust in You.
Fan the dying embers, Lord.
Stir us up and restore us to a position
of power and effectiveness.
Give us new life and new vision
so we may advance Your kingdom
in our disjointed world.
Renew Your church, O God,
and revive Your servants
so the whole earth may know of Your love.

81 and 82

*O*ur great God has heard our cry,
   and He is speaking to His church today.
He reminds us that He is the God of our world,
   the God who piloted His people through history,
      who regards His church with love and concern.
He would remind us
   that He freed us from sin's burden and guilt,
   that He responded to our pleas for deliverance
      and was present with us
      in the trials and conflicts of our lives.
He would remind us of the many times
      we neglected to listen to Him
   and how He had to allow us to hurt ourselves
      because we stubbornly chose our own course.
He reiterates His promise to meet our needs
      and to enrich our lives
         as we rely on Him for grace and strength.
He diagnoses our sickness even today
      and points us to His purpose for our existence.

We have become complacent
      in our structures and institutions.
We have been subtly diverted
      from His will and purposes in our world.
We have selfishly interpreted His Word
      to fit our schemes and carry out our intents.
We have clutched at God to pacify and sustain us
      even while we remain insensitive to the
         suffering world around us.

Now God is speaking again,
in judgment as well as with promise.
He is reaching out to restore us to Himself
and to renew our vision for His world.
"How long will you ignore
My oppressed and dispossessed children,
their cries for liberty and justice?"
our God is saying to the church.
"Why do people go hungry around you
while you abound in gifts from My hand?
You are My children and My servants,
My representatives in a fractured world.
I can reach those sick, needy, loveless,
and lonely creatures only through you.
This is the reason I have given you so much,
that you may share it with others."

Help us, O God,
to return to Your purposes for Your church,
to recognize all Your creatures as Your subjects,
to remember that the world belongs to You.
May Your great love and grace flood our lives
and overflow to touch with healing
the lives of every one of Your children.

You are in our world, O God.
May we serve You here by ministering
to the needs of those around us.

I am so depressed tonight, O God.
I feel like I am the sole target
    of an enemy barrage—
        like all the demons of hell are bent
            on damning my soul for eternity.

I remember Your precious promises,
    but I do not witness their fulfillment.
I talk to people about Your love,
    and they drown my zeal with scorn.
I step forth to carry out Your will,
    but I feel no sense of accomplishment.
I mouth words, wave my arms,
    and beat the air in fruitless endeavor.
Then I fall like a wounded warrior,
    bone-weary, defeated, and lonely.
And I wonder if You are truly my God
    and if I am really Your child.

Consume, O God, these demons that depress,
    these enemies that plague my soul.
May the whirlwind of Your Spirit
    sweep them out of my life forever.
May I awaken with a heart full of joy
    and with the strength and courage
        to walk straight and secure
            in the dangerous
                and difficult paths before me.

84

O God, the center of Your will
    is truly the place of fulfillment.
I long continuously
        for the peace and security of walking with You.
Therein lies the sole purpose and meaning for my life.

Even the birds of the air
        and the animals that inhabit land and sea
        abide within Your orbit and plan for them.
Thus it is that men and women
        who follow Your course for them
        are forever blessed.

How enriched are those
        who draw their power from You,
        whose hearts are focused on You!
Even as they wend their way
        through this fractured world,
        they become springs of healing,
            reservoirs of strength,
        to the sick, weak, and empty lives
            they touch around them.

O Lord, look with loving mercy upon those
        who have placed their lives in Your hands.
Just one day in the center of Your will
        is incomparably better than a thousand
            spent in the pursuit

of self-centered aims and objectives.
It is more fulfilling to be an underpaid clerk
        in the service of my God
        than to be the owner and director
            of some huge, wealthy enterprise.

O God, nothing that is truly good and worthwhile
        is withheld from those who walk
            within Your will.
The person who trusts You is very rich indeed.

85

O God, You indeed have been good to us.
You have prospered our land.
You have opened Your heart to us in love.
You have forgiven our sins
    and adopted us as Your sons and daughters.

But our country is in turmoil.
We no longer have confidence in our leaders.
Some segments of society feel
    disenfranchised and display their
    displeasure in open revolt.
Our young people spill blood
    in turf wars and over drugs.
People are turning away from You
    only to be ensnared
      by false doctrines
      and godless philosophies.

We know that You have not turned away from us.
You touch with joy and peace
    the hearts that belong to You.
You stand ready to show Your salvation.
    to all who will trust in You.
As we speak to You in faith,
    You respond with loving concern.
You will give us what is good
    and will prosper us
      with gifts from Your hand.

You are holy and just.
You love Your children and will guide them
in Your course for their lives.

Renew our faith, O God.
Forgive our many failures and infidelities.
May our land continue to be a place
where we are free to love and serve You.

86

O Lord, my prayer to You always comes
out of a life full of need.
I am Your servant;
I am trying to represent You.
I need Your support for every step I take.
How gracious You are to hear my plea
and respond to my cry
and pour out Your forgiving love upon me!

People are so foolish
about the things they love and worship.
You alone are God,
and You alone possess the healing grace
that can support and sustain fickle hearts.
Continue to lead me in Your course for my life.
Enable me to walk, body and soul,
in loving obedience to You.
Then I shall glorify You forever,
and my life shall be
a continual thankoffering to You.

I find the daily journey
not only difficult but painful.
There are forces within me and around me
that overpower me.
But You are a loving and patient God.
Continue to have mercy upon me,
to stir me from the doldrums of sin,

to deliver me from selfish involvements,
to forgive my sins and failures,
to shore up the weak places in my life.
Help me
feel Your loving acceptance
and reflect to others
the joy of being Your child and servant.

87

This world is God's world.
And our great God loves the world that He made
and the people He created to inhabit it.
Living in teeming cities or remote villages,
they are all God's people,
and His love embraces each and every one.

Not all the men and women of this world
are citizens of the kingdom of God.
The people who shun His redeeming love
cannot inhabit the city of eternal light.
They become the children of darkness.
They shall wander forever
through the limitless spaces of nothingness.

The sons and daughters of God enjoy
a close relationship with their
Father and Creator.
They walk in obedience to His will and Word.
They shall dwell together in joy
and shall sing and dance
in continuous celebration
in that beautiful city
beyond the boundaries and borders
of this present world.

O God, I need You every day that I exist
    and every night that I pass through.
Never turn Your face from me, O Lord,
    for my life is a continuous plea for help.

My life is one long series of conflicts and defeats,
    and they only increase as I near its end.
My ultimate destiny is a hole in the ground,
    but even now I am as good as dead.
Without strength, forsaken,
        shunned by those around me,
    I feel as if I were separated forever from You.
I am assailed by afflictions,
        attacked by obsessions,
        and all but forgotten by God and human beings.

And yet I continue to cry out to You.
Even while the assaults of this life
        and the fear of death
    surround me and close in on me,
    I look to You for some ray of hope.

Good Lord, where are You?
Is there nothing within me worth saving?

89

I feel like singing this morning, O Lord.
I feel like telling everyone around me
    how great You are.
If only they could know the depths of Your love
    and Your eternal concern for those
        who follow You!
But my songs are so often off-key.
My speech is so inadequate.
I simply cannot express what I feel,
    what I know to be true about Your love
        for Your creatures upon this world.

But even the songs of the birds
    proclaim Your praises.
The heavens and the earth beneath them,
        the trees that reach toward You,
        the flowers that glow in colorful beauty,
        the green hills and soaring mountains,
        the valleys and the plains,
        the lakes and the rivers,
        the great oceans that pound the shores—
    they proclaim Your greatness, O God,
    and Your love for Your human creatures
    throughout this world.

How glorious it is to be alive, O Lord!
May every breath of my body,
    every beat of my heart,
        be dedicated to Your praise and glory.

O God, You have always been God.
Long before the earth was formed,
    long after it ceases to exist,
    You have been and You shall always be.

With You there is no beginning or end;
    time is not measured by decades or centuries.
Our lives, so precious and important to us,
    are only fleeting shadows to You.
And they are full of trouble and conflict
    and marked by sin and failure.

O God, break into our short span of existence
    with Your eternal love and grace.
Intersperse our days of despair
    with hours of joy.
Enable us
    to see Your will and purpose
      for our presence here
    and to discover some meaning
      for our brief, trouble-fraught
        appearance in this world.
Imprint on us Your brand of ownership,
    and place us
      within Your plan and objective for our lives.

91

Those who focus their faith on God,
    who find their security in Him,
    do not have to live in fear.
They are not left untouched
        by the tempests of this life,
    and they may be wounded
        by the onslaughts of evil,
    but their great God does not leave them
    to suffer these things alone.
The Lord cares for His own and delivers them
    even in the midst of the conflicts
        that plague them.

If God is truly your God,
    you do not have to be afraid
        of the enemy that threatens
            or the affliction that lays you low.
Men and women all around you may fall,
        never to rise again,
    but the Lord is by your side
        to raise you to your feet
        and to lead You to ultimate victory.

Even the ministering spirits of His invisible world
        watch over you.
They will not let anything hurt you
        except by God's loving permission
        and through His eternal concern.

Our loving God has promised:
"Because My children love Me,
    I will never let them go.
I shall feel the pain of their wounds
        and bear their hurt
    and shall transform that which is ugly
        into that which enriches and blesses.
And when they cry out in agony,
    I shall hear and answer them.
I will be close to them and will deliver them,
    and I will grant them eternal life."

92

It's a glorious feeling to be able
  to unload my heart,
  to spill out my gratitude
    in thanks to You, O God.
Morning, noon, and night,
  I want the whole world to know of Your love.
I want to shout it, to sing it,
  in every possible way
    to proclaim Your praises,
    to express my joy.

How great You are, O Lord!
Your thoughts are unfathomable,
  Your ways beyond comprehension.
And all the while, the problem of evil
  still confounds us.
We simply cannot understand
  why the ungodly appear to be so successful,
  why good fortune seems to follow those
    who defy You.
But we know their success is short-lived.
Those who refuse to turn to You will never find
  that ultimate and total fulfillment
    that is promised to the children of God.

The children of God,
    those whose lives are open to You,
    portray the wonder and beauty of Your Spirit.

They are like springs of water in a parched world.
They flourish even amid the distortions
and the ugliness around them.
Their lives are rich and productive
in a barren and desolate society.

Help us, those of us who love You, O God,
to prove to our disjointed world
that You are in our midst.

93

It may not always be apparent,
    but God does reign over our world.
He rules in majesty and might,
    and no philosophy or power
        can cast Him from His throne.

He allows us to cross up His purposes—
    even to destroy His visible creation.
But His place and His reign are eternally secure.
And so are they who put their trust in Him,
    who live by His precepts,
        and who follow His course for their lives.

It is difficult, O God, to understand
how You can ignore Your enemies
as they persist in thwarting Your purposes
and abusing Your children in this world.
They provoke me to anger, O Lord.
How can You withhold Your vengeance?

Even those of us who name Your name
and sing Your praises
are often indifferent to or careless about
the needs of those around us.
We stand indicted, Lord.
Our calloused self-centeredness has perpetuated
the wars and poverty and bigotry
that abound in our society.
We don't hate people, Lord,
we just don't really care about them.

Is it possible, O Lord, that we are Your enemies?
That we are thwarting Your purposes
and abusing Your children in this world?
We are busy with good works, Lord.
We build churches and send out missionaries
and establish schools and hospitals
and homes for the elderly.
But we don't like the poor, Lord,
or the people who can't speak our language,
or those who don't appreciate our patronizing gifts.

They frighten us when they reach out
    for the fruits of our labor,
        our affluence, our respectability,
        our right to be wealthy
        and comfortable and secure.
Sometimes, Lord, we just don't like people.
Why don't they leave us alone
    so we can love and serve You in peace?

Thank You, God, for not pouring out Your wrath
    on those who are disobedient to You.
We have been Your enemies at times.
Even while we worship
    in our comfortable sanctuaries,
    we may stand in Your way.
And thank You, God,
    because You love even Your enemies,
        and through Your chastisement
        may transform them into
        Your sons and daughters.

Strike the scales from our eyes, O Lord,
    that we may see Your handwriting on the wall
        and accept Your chastening love
        and return to You in repentance and faith.
Strike the shackles from our hearts and hands
    that we may reach out to demonstrate
        and to relate Your love
        to Your children around us.

Let us begin this day with singing.
Whether we feel like it or not,
    let us make glad sounds
        and force our tongues to articulate words
          of thanksgiving and praise.

The facts are: God is with us;
    this world and we who live in it are His;
    He loves us;
    He has adopted us as His children;
    we belong to Him.
This makes us valid, worthwhile.
We are truly significant in the eyes of our God
    despite our human feelings
        or the comments of our critics.

This may not be the way we feel this morning,
    but this is the way it is.
We don't need the plaudits of our peers—
    we have God's stamp of approval.

So let us begin this day with singing
    whether we feel like it or not.
Then we may end this day with praises
    because we know—and may even feel—
        that we shall forever be
          the objects of God's concern
          and the children of His love.

96

God is here; God is now!
It is time for celebration!
Our praises need not be confined to old songs.
Nor do we need great organs or massive choirs
    to honor His name.
Let us create new songs of praise to our God.
Let us discover new ways of proclaiming
    His greatness and glory!

The elements around us reflect His majesty.
The roaring sea and all that inhabits it,
        the wind that bends the trees,
        the creatures that fill the air and land,
        the mountains that probe our skies,
        the rivers and lakes that slake our thirst,
        the great planets and stars
            that light up our night—
all these reveal God's beauty and splendor.
And out of this comes that fashioned
        by human mind and body:
            art, architecture, music, literature,
            and the inventions of science.

Wherever one turns,
        God's power is manifested,
        God's presence is made apparent.
Let us celebrate His presence
        in our world today.

I can't even see the sun this morning.
The coastland fog has blotted out heaven's light,
    making the early hours cold and damp.
But God is here—in me and around me—
    and I will rejoice in Him.

I hear no angel choirs.
No church bells summon me to worship.
Only the thunder of four-wheel vehicles
        and the acrid odor of exhaust greet me
        as men and women rush to their unnumbered shrines
            and pursue their avaricious goals.
But God is here, and I will rejoice in Him.

I cannot see the mountains or smell the flowers
    or even hear the songs of birds.
I cannot love the people who bustle around me.
I see unhappiness and injustice and depravity.
I hear the ear-grating sounds of pain and complaint.
I feel the stifling pressures that suck me
    into the stream that rushes by my door.
But God is here—in me and around me—
    and I will rejoice in Him.

Our great God does care for His creatures.
He secures forever those who are His.
He is here—in us and around us.
Let us all rejoice in Him!

98

Men and women have proclaimed God's praises
    throughout the ages.
Now it is our turn to worship the Lord
    and to announce God's presence
       and His loving concern
       to the inhabitants of this world.
His power is as great today as it ever was.
He continues to reign over His universe
    and the creatures that move in this world.
He alone is the true God.
He offers to all men and women His salvation.
He is close to His children and servants
    and fills their hearts with joy.

Now, as His children and servants,
    let us express this joy.
With voice and musical instruments,
      with lovely melodies and joyful sounds,
    let us proclaim the glory of God.
Let us fill our homes and sanctuaries,
    our halls of learning,
    our factories and marketplaces,
    even the streets of our city,
      with sounds of celebration.
God is here; God is now!

The Lord does reign over this world!
Even when the earth quakes
and fires rage through the forests
and floods inundate the lowlands
and human beings and their creations are laid low,
God is Lord and Master over all the earth.

The Lord does reign over this world!
Even when people turn against one another
and nations engage in war
and violence and injustice are heaped
on His creatures,
God is Lord and Master over all the earth.

God's creatures bear the consequences
of their self-centeredness,
and this world is distorted by their depravity.
But the Lord forgives those who turn to Him
and makes them His children and His servants
and through them seeks to heal
this world's gaping wounds
and the hurts that people inflict upon one another.

The Lord establishes relationships with those who
call upon Him.
The priests and prophets of history
heard His voice
and followed His course for their lives.

His servants and disciples of this hour
    sense His presence
    and communicate His love and grace
    to those who reach out for Him.

The Lord does reign over this world!
He is Lord and Master over all the earth.

$\mathcal{B}$reak forth
    into exclamations of joy and gladness,
    you who serve the Lord!

God is not dead! He is ever our God!
He made us, we belong to Him;
    we are His children and servants.
And His love for us never runs out;
    His care and concern for us will go on forever.

Let the world see our manifestations of joy!
Let us lift up our voices in songs of praise
    and surrender our lives
        as continual offerings of thanksgiving!
Let us bless His name forever!

101

O God, I love those hymns
    that speak of loyalty and justice,
    those prayers for the deprived and oppressed—
    even while I deprive and oppress my fellow persons
    through my apathy and egocentricity.

I embrace the old creeds that tell of Your love
        and the commandments that instruct me
        to reflect that love to others—
    even while I turn inward
    and allow bigotry and prejudice
        to color my relationships
        with those outside my private little club.
I treasure those promises I made in the sanctuary,
        those vows and solemn pledges before the altar—
    even while I flirt with this world's gods
        and bow before manmade shrines.
I decry the distortions of our world,
        the poverty and pain and indignities
        suffered by multitudes
        of this world's citizens—
    even while I stand aloof
        and wait for people's sorry needs
        to be met by others
    and brazenly oppose those remedies
        that may result in personal deprivation.
I avoid the sinner
        and belittle the proud

and stand clear of cheaters and liars
and choose as my companions
the qualified and respected
members of my society.
And all the while I claim to be Your child
and to walk in Your ways.

Have mercy upon me, O God,
for I am a selfish and self-centered creature!

102

Good Lord, where are You?
If You really do exist,
    why don't You come out of hiding and
        do something about this creature in distress?

I am physically weary.
I am mentally depressed.
I am spiritually defeated.
I can't eat, can't sleep.
I am like garbage,
    discarded refuse in the back alley;
    like yesterday's newspaper,
        shuffled around by the wind.
I feel like some sort of zombie,
    some nonentity,
    some nothing that people,
        if they acknowledged me,
    would only curse.
I eat crow and drink gall.
Now even You have tossed me aside
    like some moth-eaten garment
        that no one could possibly want.

But the prophets have proclaimed Your name,
    and the Scriptures declare Your mercy,
    and the saints pass on Your promises.
You do reign over our world, they say.
    You do show concern

for the poor clods of this earth.
Good Lord, prove it!
Look down from wherever You are
on Your creatures wallowing in wretchedness.
Deliver us, O God, set us free!

I must take comfort in Your everlastingness—
that You, who outlive seasons and centuries,
who have blessed the saints of the past,
can also care for Your servants
in this fearful hour.
For Your years have no end
nor do the lives of those who trust in You.

103

My heart bursts with praises to God;
  every fiber of my being reaches out in rejoicing!
How can I ever forget His many blessings?
    He forgives all my sins;
    He touches my afflictions with healing;
    He snatches me back
      from the gaping jaws of hell;
    He covers me with concern and love;
    He fulfills my deepest desires and gives me
      meaning for life and purpose for living.

God is a God of judgment and justice,
    but He sides with those who need His help.
He is angry with those
      who persistently rebel against Him,
    but He pours out His love
      on those who turn to Him.
He does not give us our just deserts
    or pay us what we well deserve.
He is grieved when we so miserably fail,
    but He quickly draws us to His forgiving heart
      and accepts us just as if it never happened.
He looks with tenderness
      at His faltering children;
    He knows and understands our fallible natures.

God's human creatures are pitiful
      pictures of weakness.

Now and then one will,
     like a streaking meteor,
     blaze out across the skies of time
          only to become a smoking cinder
          at the end of the short journey.
But those who are joined
          to God's loving will and purposes
     become the objects
          of His eternal mercy and righteousness.

Rejoice with me
     you who are His invisible servants
     and you who hear and obey His voice.
Shout His praises
     you who are His children
     and you who serve
          as His ministers and priests.
There is no time for despair and discouragement.
Whoever and wherever you are,
     lift your hearts in praises to God.

104

O Lord, how great and all-powerful You are!
And how beautiful is the world You created
    for our habitation!
Even before Adam was brought forth from the dust,
    or Eve was brought forth from Adam's rib,
    You prepared for them a place
        in which to live and grow.
And everything they saw around them
    reflected the beauty and power
        of the living God.

There was clean air.
Pure water from snowcapped mountains
    flowed through green valleys
    and gathered together in great lakes.
The skies shone with a million lights.
The land brought forth flowers and fruits
    to delight the eye and palate of God's creatures.
And every part of the land
    and the waters that covered the land
    and the skies that looked down on the land
        were filled with uncountable forms of life;
    the world was vibrant and alive.

Your power and Your beauty were spread
        throughout the universe,
    but it was only upon the heart of
        human creatures that You imprinted Your image.

And these creatures,
    in their short stay on this world,
    were appointed to be Your coworkers
        in the ever-continuing process of creation.
Your creative activity has never ceased.
It continues in and through their lives.

Limited and lowly as Your human creatures are,
    their minds and their hands are assigned
        to control Your life-giving process
    and to direct the maintenance and
        replenishment of the earth
    that life might be given and sustained
        throughout the world.

O Lord, how great and all-powerful You are!
And how beautiful is the world You created
    for our habitation!

*H*ow great is my God,
and how I love to sing His praises!
Whereas I am often frightened
when I think about the future
and confused and disturbed
by the rapidly changing world around me,
my heart is secured and made glad
when I remember how God has cared for me
throughout the past.

When I came from my mother's womb,
God's hand was on me.
Through parents and people who cared,
He loved and sheltered me
and set me on His course for my life.
Through illness and accident,
my God has sustained me.
Around pitfalls and precipices
He has safely led me.
When I became rebellious
and struck out on my own,
He waited patiently for me to return.
When I fell on my face in weakness and failure,
He gently set me on my feet again.
He did not always prevent me from hurting myself,
but He comforted me and healed my wounds.
Even out of the broken pieces of my defeats,
He created a vessel of beauty and usefulness.

Through trials and errors, failures and successes,
    my God has cared for me.
From infancy to adulthood,
    He has never let me go.
His love has led me—or carried me—
    through the valleys of sorrow
        and the highlands of joy,
    through times of want
        and years of abundance.
He has bridged impassable rivers
    and moved impossible mountains.
Sometimes through me,
        sometimes despite me,
    He seeks to accomplish His purposes in my life.

He has kept me through the stormy past;
    He will secure and guide me
        through the perilous future.
I never need to be afraid,
    no matter how uncertain
        the months or years ahead of me.
How great is my God,
    and how I love to sing His praises!

106

I praise God today!
How exciting it is to be His child and servant!
What amazes me
    is the manner in which He makes
      hay out of the straw and stubble
    of my feeble efforts and foolish errors.

This is the way God deals with all His children.
We have so often fallen away from His love
    and accepted His gifts
      without respect or concern for the Giver.
We spout gratitude
    when some great deliverance
      comes our way:
    a successful surgery, a return to health,
    a financial bonus, a debt erased,
    a reconciliation with a loved one.
But when the crisis passes and calm is restored,
    we return to our old tricks,
      walk in our old ways,
      pursue our self-centered goals,
    with little concern for God's
      way and will for our lives.

We rejoice when God smiles on us,
    and sound off
      about how good and gracious He is.
But when we meet up with hard times

or become enslaved
to the boredom of the daily routine,
we lapse into grumbling and griping
    and act as if God were a million miles away.

How loving and patient is my God!
Even when I fail Him,
    He never fails to love and care for me.
I so often limit Him
    with my inability to trust Him,
    my unwillingness to obey Him,
    my apathy, my self-concern,
    or my pursuit of the foolish
        goals and ambitions of this life.
And yet my God never ceases to pursue me,
    to draw me back into His circle of love,
    and to carry out His purposes
        even through the failures and defeats
        of my life.

How I praise God today!
How I pray that He may find pleasure
    in my love for Him!

107

Those who have experienced
the redemption of God
and know what it means
to be reconciled to Him
ought to dedicate their lives to serving Him
and their voices to proclaiming
to the world His loving grace.

Some of you have known
the meaning of emptiness and loneliness.
You have drunk from many wells
and sipped honey from many flowers
and stumbled into many blind alleys
in your search for fulfillment.
But your hearts remained empty and unsatisfied.
Then you faced up to God
and His claim on you,
and you discovered purpose and objective
for your lives.
Don't keep it to yourselves!
Tell it to the world!
Proclaim in word and deed
the wonderful works of a loving God.
Let others know that He is able
to fill their emptiness and satiate
their hunger.

Some of you have endured the long nights
of suffocating darkness.
You know well the dregs of depression,

the power of obsession,
the clutch of despair and frustration.
You fell on your faces in defeat,
and no one seemed to care.
Then in desperation you cried out
to God in your misery;
and He flooded your lives with light and hope.
Thank God! It is by His eternal love
that you are delivered.
Tell others about His power to deliver them
from that which binds them or blinds them.

Some of you have followed
sin's cruel consequences
into the crucible of sickness and pain.
You were led to the very brink of destruction.
Then you turned to God in your great distress,
and He touched you with His healing
and delivered you from your afflictions.
Rejoice in God! Let your praises ascend to Him!
Proclaim His healing grace
to others who may be ready to listen.

Some of you have set out in joyous abandon
to find your happiness in the streets
and marketplaces of the world.
But you became lost and disillusioned and afraid.
The exciting landscape became a devouring monster
that threatened to dehumanize and destroy you.

You cried out for help,
　　　and you found that God was there
　　　among the milling masses.

He restored courage to your hearts
　　　and meaning to your lives.
You discovered purpose
　　　and validity and significance
　　　　　in the loving acceptance of your God.
Let the multitudes hear
　　　about your discovery!
Let them know that God is near
　　　that they may rejoice
　　　　　in His everlasting and ever-present love.
It is the lack of God in people's lives
　　　that dries them up and turns them into dust.
It is God's presence and acceptance
　　　that turns on the lights
　　　and floods the dark corridors that led nowhere
　　　and transforms them into warm rooms
　　　where one may live
　　　　　in joy and fulfillment.
It is the acknowledgment of a loving God
　　　that makes the forbidding world a place
　　　　　to live in
　　　and its God-fearing inhabitants
　　　　　glowing reflections of His eternal concern.

Great God, be it crowded street or solitary mountaintop,
    make it my pulpit
      from which to proclaim Your praises
    and my workbench from which to transmit
      Your love to the lives of lonely men and women.

108

My heart is glad today, O God,
  and I am determined to serve You!
I celebrate Your presence.
I glory in Your love for me.
I sing Your praises
  and yearn to proclaim Your loving concern to all.

The people I travel with have little feeling for You.
They act as if You do not exist.
They are empty.
Their lives have little meaning or purpose.
They bounce about in a vacuum,
  the deepest longings of their hearts unfulfilled.

I know to whom I belong,
  and I know where I am going.
I know that You are my Lord
  and that You will accompany me
    as I walk the streets of the city and
      mingle with its groping inhabitants.

I pray, O Lord, that You will use me,
  that through my fumbling efforts
    You will touch some soul with healing and love.

My heart is glad today, O God.
Grant that I may communicate to others
  some measure of this eternal joy.

O God, I have been taught to believe
 that You are God of our world.
It has been drummed into my head
 by the preachers of my youth,
 by parents, teachers, and self-appointed apostles.
"God holds the reins," they say.
"He will have the last word," they claim.

I've honestly tried to believe it.
And with tongue in cheek,
 I've sounded off to others
 about Your power and Your promises.
Maybe they sensed my disbelief.
It may be that they just habitually accepted
 or unthinkingly nodded assent
 to my platitudes and pronouncements.
How can I really believe in Your omnipotence
 unless I look the other way
 when tragedy befalls
 or close my eyes to the agony and ugliness
 on all sides of me?

I cannot believe You inflict pain on Your creatures.
I realize that our suffering is
 the consequence of our own sinful selfishness.
But what about the babies born
 with two strikes against them?
 the children killed because they're inconvenient?
 the grisly slaughter on gang turf,
 battlefield, highways?

the diseases that kill without cause?
the destruction of thousands when the earth
    shifts and breaks under them?
the pressures and indignities
    forced on ethnic minorities?
What about this, O God?
How can I explain this to my skeptical friends
    or even to myself?

Is it possibly true, O God,
    that You really aren't omnipotent?
    that this fractured world isn't
        in the palm of Your hand?
    that Your great power is limited
        when it comes to this distorted planet
            and its sin-ridden inhabitants?

O God, the basis of all being,
    my ultimate and eternal concern,
    I know that You are not floating out there
        over and above our ball of clay.
You are in our world.
You are among Your creatures,
    inscrutable, indefinable,
        great in majesty and splendor.
You bring beauty out of ugliness.
Out of the ashes of our sickness and suffering,
    You bring forth new creations.
I never want to define You, O God,

for I cannot worship what I comprehend.
But I pray for Your grace to stand firm
    despite my nagging doubts
and to praise You in time of adversity.

God spoke to me today.
He broke through my childish doubts
    with words of comfort and assurance.
"Hang in there; sit tight;
       stick to My course for your life," He said,
     "I will not let you down."

He reminded me of how He cared for past saints,
    how He watched over them and kept them
      through their hours of suffering
        and uncertainty.
He reviewed for me my own life,
    His loving concern through the days of my youth.
He restated for me my commission and
     appointment,
    His trust in me as His servant
     in this sin-filled world.
He reiterated His gracious promises to stand by me,
    to empower and support me
     in the conflicts that await.

I know that God is with me today—
    just as surely as He was with His saints of old.
I have no reason to fear or doubt
    the eternal love and presence of my Lord.

*M*y heart is full today.
I am so grateful
    for all that God has done for me.
As I crawl out of my corner
      of depression and self-pity
    and look around me, I see
      how great my God is.
I cannot see Him,
    but I can see the works of His hands.
He is a merciful and loving God.
How tenderly He deals with those
    whose hearts are open to Him!
He is a righteous and faithful God.
His promises and precepts are forever.
He is a majestic and powerful God.
He created me and sustains me day to day.
He is a forgiving God.
He takes me back to His loving heart
    when I go astray.
He is in this world today.
And those who recognize and belong to Him
    are building on foundations
      that are eternally secure.
How grateful I am to my God today!

112

What about those people who trust in God
and are committed to His will and purposes?

They are people who are rich indeed.
Even amid the circumstances of poverty,
    the wealth and blessings of God
      are within their reach.
They are people with purpose and meaning in their lives.
Even amid the disorder and void
    of this temporal existence,
     they are aware of God's concern and love for them.
They are people who walk unafraid.
The threats of violence or prophecies of doom
    do not detract from their validity
      nor alter their course.
They are people who relate to those around them.
They identify with others
    in their sorrows and complaints
   and share with them their lives and gifts.

They are people who are truly happy
    and through whom our God works
      His purposes in this world today.

How *great and glorious is our God!*
From hour to hour, from day to day,
    our lives ought to overflow
      with praise and gratitude.
It is amazing, even fantastic,
    how our God permeates every facet of our lives
      and works His purposes
        despite our human faults and failures.

He creates beauty out of the dust
    of our fallen natures.
Out of the ashes of our failures
    He brings forth meaning and purpose.
He exalts the humble and enriches the poor.
He transforms our weaknesses
    into channels of strength.
Our emptiness becomes
    a vessel of His fullness,
    our spiritual poverty
      the basis for His eternal grace.
Our errors and mistakes
    are stepping-stones to success.
Our defeats are only incidents
    on the road to victory.

But this is God's doing, not ours.
How great and glorious is our God!

114 and 115

We fear, O God, for our country
and the tragic indifference that is demonstrated
toward You and Your purposes.
We have built great sanctuaries and memorials
in Your honor.
We have established innumerable church bodies
that presume to glorify and serve You.
We have respectfully imprinted Your name
on our coins
and properly credited You
in our founding principles.
Our leaders generally call on You to guide them
in the most critical decisions
they must make.
A remnant of our populace gathers occasionally
to sing Your praises and profess its faith.
There are even special days
when we count our blessings
and conduct services of thanksgiving.

But the sanctuaries we build do not always glorify You.
They often become soundproof fortresses
that block out the sounds of suffering
that echo throughout the world around them.
Our numerous church bodies turn into vain attempts
to box You into human ideas
and concepts of divinity.
The coins that bear Your name are dedicated

to the pursuit of our selfish ambitions
and the acquisition of material wealth.
Our founding principles are interpreted to
benefit the powerful and oppress the weak.
Our laws sometimes contradict and oppose Your law
in the consciences and convictions
of Your children.
Our leaders call on You to bless their intentions
rather than to reveal Your plans
in the way they govern.
And those who do gather to sing Your praises
are seldom committed to anyone or anything
unless it is comfortable and convenient
for their purposes.

And yet, O Lord, we pray
that You will not give up on us.
We have selfishly clutched at Your great blessings
and abused the wealth You have put
into our hands.
We have gathered for ourselves
while countless millions
of this world's creatures have died
with their needs unfulfilled.
We have foolishly ignored You to worship the things
that have come from Your hands.
We confess our rebelliousness and selfishness,

O Lord,
and pray that You will spare us.
Spare us that you might renew us
and save us
and use us to share Your blessings
with Your human creatures in every land.
You dealt mercifully with Your ungrateful children
throughout history.
We pray that You will deal patiently and lovingly
with us,
that You will transform our words into actions
and our shallow platitudes into genuine praises
that will glorify and serve You
in all the world.

_116_

I know that God is here.
I know this because,
      with my soul bare and my body naked before Him,
    He looked on me with love
      and responded to my cry for help.

There was a time when I didn't care!
I was not aware of any particular need for Him.
But then I hit bottom.
Death itself reached out to embrace me.
There was no one else to turn to.
I cried out to God in my desperation.
I could almost feel His invisible hand
      encircle me and draw me to Himself.

Now I am convinced.
God is here, and I shall trust Him forever.
I will no longer wait for pain or suffering
      to drive me to Him.
I will walk in His course for my life.
I am committed to His purposes,
      and I intend to carry out that commitment.

I can never repay God for His ever-present love.
I can only dedicate my life to praising Him
      and to serving Him wherever I may be.
I am His servant and His child; I shall love Him forever.
I shall proclaim to all the world: "God is in our midst."

117 *and* 118

O God, I am thoroughly frightened when I see
the things that are happening around me.
And when I dare to peer into the future,
I become very nervous as I consider
what may happen to me and my world.

I do remember Your many promises.
I keep telling myself:
"With the Lord on my side,
I do not have to be afraid;
what can anyone do to me?"
But when I see the old foundations crumbling
and the old certainties
and securities giving way,
I feel as if I am falling with no one
to catch me
or that my ship has broken loose
from its anchor, leaving me
at the mercy of a tempestuous sea.

Our world has slipped its moorings:
our population threatens to overwhelm us;
our waste products are about to smother us;
our modern weapons are capable
of obliterating us;
diseases run rampant, claiming
innocent lives.
Because we are incapable of loving and living
for one another,

we are about to be destroyed
by our own self-centeredness
and to turn the beautiful world You have given us
into a wasted and desolate planet.
It all seems so unreal,
and I feel so small and insignificant
in such a world.
And sometimes it seems, O God,
that even You have left us to our own devices
and have given us up for lost.
Or, I wonder, are You about to wind up history?
Is Your purpose for our world
about to be consummated?

You do speak to my fears, O Lord.
You offer no guarantees
about the future of the world,
but You have assured me that my status
as Your beloved child is eternal.
Whatever happens to my world,
You will never let me go.
You have set me free from fear
and will keep me safe and secure
through all the storms
that rage around me.
You are my God;
whatever happens to the world,
I will celebrate Your love forever.

119

O God, I want so much to please You,
   to walk in Your ways
   and to carry out Your purposes.
Nothing is as important to me
   as being in the center of Your will
      and living within Your design for my life.

While others may find their fulfillment
   in the acquisition of wealth
      or the accumulation of things,
   in doing something better than everyone else,
      or in the plaudits of their peers,
   my foremost desire is
      to be the object of Your love
      and to be Your child and servant forever.

Not only have You fashioned me with Your hands,
      O Lord,
   and created me for Your purposes,
   You have stamped Your image on my heart.
Therefore my deepest longings are met only in You
   and in the dedication of my life
      to the accomplishment of Your objectives.

How can I live a life that is pleasing to You,
      O Lord?
My instincts are earthbound.
The transitory delights of this life
   tantalize and tempt me.
My insatiable longings
   and desperate attempts to please You
      are thwarted by the innumerable

enemies of my soul.
I fail so often to do what I really want to do,
     to attain what I strive for,
     to grasp what I reach for,
    and I fall back in shame
     and am flattened in despair.

You do forgive me when I fail, O Lord,
    and You set me on my feet again.
You have promised to strengthen me
    and to sustain me in my daily conflicts.
Now I pray for the wisdom to discern Your will
    and the grace to carry it out
     in the difficult days before me.
You have shown me how much You love me, Lord;
    now show me how to love You.
Your standards for me are clear.
I am to translate Your love into terms
     that others can comprehend,
    to demonstrate it before my fellow beings.
I can truly love You only as I proceed
    to love Your children in this world.
I can serve You only as I commit my life to service
    on behalf of my brothers and sisters.
I can offer sacrifices to You only as
    I sacrifice to meet my neighbor's need.
This is Your law and standard,
    Your design and will for my life.
This is the way in which I will be pleasing to You.

I do love You, O God,
    and Your will for me is the delight of my heart.

I have a sincere love for many people
    who cross my path,
    and I rejoice in the privilege of serving them.
And yet, O Lord, there are so many people
    whom I do not love.
The demons of bigotry and apathy,
    jealousy and selfishness,
        plague my soul and numb my sensitivities.
They stay my hand from reaching out
    to help others.
I sin against You when I sin against them,
    and I need to be restored and renewed
        by Your loving touch.

How I praise You, O Lord,
    because You love me even when I fail
    to respond in loving obedience!
Whereas I cannot comprehend You,
    You do understand me,
    and You continue to hold me
        within Your loving embrace.
While I fall short of my sincere intentions
        to abide within Your will for me,
    Your promises are eternally secure,
    and You tenderly and patiently
        rekindle the fires within me and empower me
        to do that which I cannot do by myself.

I love You, O God,
    and I gladly accept Your will and purpose

for my life.
Now bless me and guide me
and grant me the grace
to walk within Your will and purpose
and have the joy of knowing
that I am pleasing to You.

120

I am distressed, O Lord,
>by the attitudes and actions of those
>>who claim to honor Your name
>>>and to live within Your purposes.

They don't really listen to Your Word.
They appear to be following some other god,
>or they are simply taking the path
>>of least resistance.
They assume that their wishes are Your will,
>that the crowd they travel with
>or the nations that govern them
>>are righteously carrying out Your objectives
>>>despite their ungodly
>>>means and methods.

How long, O Lord, must I dwell
>in a world that breeds violence
>and amongst people that engage in war?

Teach me, O God, how to be a peacemaker,
>how to confront violence with love,
>how to courageously and patiently promote
>>Your will and Your Word
>>>among the hostile and angry masses.

Where should I look for help in my need?
To majestic mountain peaks that probe our skies
    or to giants of industry that clog our land?
To satellites that circle our world
    or to computers that store our knowledge?

The answer to my problems
        and the fulfillment of my needs
    must come from God Himself,
        from Him who created skies and mountains
        and men and women to dwell in their midst.
He is a great God who knows our every desire,
        whose watchful eye is upon us night and day.
We can make no move without His knowledge.
His concern for His children is constant,
    His love for them eternal.

And thus the Lord will keep you,
    shielding you from the forces of evil
    as a shade tree shields you
        from the rays of the blazing sun.

He does care for you,
    and He will fight with you
        against the enemies of your soul.
Whether you are coming or going,
    He knows the course you take,
        and He will go before you.

122 and 123

How good it is to enter the sanctuary of the Lord!
I know that God is not confined
within our four-walled creations,
nor is He attached to altars and brass symbols.
And yet, in the beauty and quietness of God's house,
I find His presence very real and fulfilling.

God is with me and around me
even as I make my way
through the concrete and steel jungles
of the cold and unfriendly city.

He is present even behind the anonymous faces
of the rushing crowds elbowing their way
to their respective destinations.
I find Him in the hearts and lives of His children
who infiltrate the masses
and run His errands
and fulfill His purposes
in the course of their daily duties.
I cannot outrun or evade my God.
He goes before me and follows closely behind me.
He will keep me and sustain me wherever I am.

And yet I rejoice as I enter His sanctuary
and mingle with those who honor His name
and seek His grace.

There, shielded from the screaming tensions
    and ear-splitting sounds of the city,
   in the company of those who love one another,
    I happily open my heart
      to the loving mercy of God.

124 and 125

What cowards we are,
    we who claim to be the sons and daughters of God!
How insipid is our faith
    in an insecure and faithless world!
The pressures increase.
The old props fall away.
Many of the old traditions and standards
    we held so dear are no longer relevant
        in our rapidly changing society.
Even the proclamations and exhortations,
    the prophecies and promises,
        that excited and supported us in our youth
        sound hollow and empty and frightfully
        inadequate in these times in which we live.
The little boxes we wrapped around our God
        are breaking up;
    we can no longer hold on to Him in our
        expanding, exploding universe.

Though we cannot hold on to God,
    He does hold on to us.
Those who trust in the true God are more secure
    than the great mountains that rise above the
        clouds that cover us.
Though everything changes around us,
    our great God cannot be changed.
Though the sands may shift and
    even our institutions and governments

and the ideals and aspirations of
   men and women give way,
our great God is not subject to the impermanence
of our temporal world.
Though the storm sweeps over us,
   our relationship with our loving God is forever.

What cowards we are, we who claim to be the
   sons and daughters of God!
We don't have to be afraid.
Let us have faith in God!

Let us begin this day with rejoicing!
Let us acknowledge our Lord's love and concern
and allow our bodies to break forth
into happy hilarity!
Let us give our nerves and muscles
the healthy exercise of laughter!
The Lord has done such wonderful things for us;
let us be glad!

The day before us is uncertain.
We don't know what we will encounter on our way.
While we rejoice with those who rejoice,
we shall also weep with those who suffer.
While we may be surprised by heavenly bliss,
we may also pass through corridors of darkness.
Wherever we go, we go forth as children and servants
of the living God,
and we go forth to touch the lives of men and women
with His healing love.

Let us begin this day with rejoicing
and return to our homes with gladness!

127 and 128

Those human creatures who struggle for significance
 apart from God's will and purposes
  struggle in vain.
They build homes and institutions;
 they acquire property and possessions;
 they crowd the land with their clutter
  of questionable achievements;
 they fill the better part of every day
  with self-centered activities;
 they strive constantly to get to the top.
And all the while, worth and value
  are within their reach or very close to them.
They possess a precious gift from God
 that comes in some measure to all people.

There are visible evidences of a man and woman's worth:
 the children they beget,
 their ability to supply their family's needs
  through daily labor.
But even beyond this and long before this,
 a person's true worth was established
  by God Himself.

129

O God, I get awfully tired of static.
I am fed up with the flack that comes my way
   from those I am trying to serve.
It seems that they suspect or misinterpret
   or question my motives or authority
      in everything I do or say.
I think people enjoy putting me down.
I just can't get them off my back.

Do I have to constantly live
   with this sort of thing, O Lord?
What about this joy that is promised to those
   who are Your servants and ministers?

Forgive me for my unworthy thoughts, O Lord.
Overlook my vicious complaints.
   Fill my heart with Your love
      so I will respond in love
         even toward those who do not love me.
Enable me, O Lord, to find my joy in You
   and to reflect that joy to the unresponsive,
      reactionary, disagreeable people
         who do not like me very much.

130

O God, tonight I seek You
 with a heart full of guilt
 and a mind full of bewilderment
  and frustration.
You have heard me before
 and responded with grace and mercy.
Now I seek You again.

I know I am guilty, O God.
But if You kept account of people's
  failings and fallings,
  no one could ever face You.
I reach for You
 because You look with loving mercy
  on my wretched soul.
You will accept me and forgive me
 and reinstate me in Your purposes.

It is no wonder that I return again and again to God.
I long for His forgiveness and acceptance
 more than the night watchman longs
  for the dawn of day.

Thus I plead with you to focus your faith on God.
You will find love there—and salvation.
And He will cleanse you of your sin
 and restore you to His loving heart.

131

O God, I have failed
    because I expected too much of myself.
I have fallen
        because I focused too much on success
            and reckoned too little with my own humanity.

It is time that I still my restless heart
        and quiet my overambitious spirit.

It is far better that I center my aspirations
        on God and His will for my life.

*W*e remember, O Lord,
> those past saints who suffered sorely
>> on Your behalf.

In obedience to You, they endured persecution—
> even torture and death.

In their heroic determination to live by Your will
>> and to remain in Your course for their lives,
> they proclaimed and demonstrated Your Word
>> to this world's masses.

We remember, O Lord,
> and we are ashamed of our insipid faith,
>> our cowardice,
>>> our fear of offending those with power over us
>>>> and of being despised by those around us.

Make us aware, O Lord,
> of Your children who even today
> are suffering for their faith,
> who even in our great country
>> have the courage to place Your will
>>> above the laws of the state
> and are subjected to
>> the indignities of imprisonment,
>> the scorn of their peers,
>> and even the compassionless criticisms
> of many of us who honor Your name.

We confess, O Lord,
    our lack of courage and understanding.
We pray for Your blessing on those who suffer,
    that You will not forget them
      in their hour of trial
    and that You will not turn Your face from them
      in their lonely hours of doubt and pain.

Visit them with joy; empower them with Your Spirit;
    watch over and care for them.
May the influence of their courageous convictions
    shake us out of our lethargy,
    move us from the fringes of fear and indecision
      into the center of Your will.
    Empower us with Your grace
      to carry on Your purposes
        despite the consequences
        that may come our way.

133 *and* 134

O God, how precious it is for us
and how pleasing it must be to You
when Your children and servants learn
how to live and work together in unity!

It is in the measure that we do this
that we begin to resemble You
and to carry out more effectively Your purposes
in our disjointed and discordant world.
Come, let us bless His name together,
rejoice in His loving concern for us,
declare His worth to all creatures,
and walk in obedience to His will.

The same God made heaven and earth
and all of us who dwell here.
Let us worship and serve Him together.

135

Despite the depressing conditions of our world
 and the distortions of our society,
  or even the problems and conflicts of our lives,
 let us take time to praise the Lord.

We who gather for services of worship,
 let us come together to celebrate God's presence
 and to praise Him for His great gifts.
As we take our place in our workday world,
 let us begin by praising the Lord.
When we meet with our family and friends,
 let us unite our voices in praises to the Lord.
Farmers who labor alone with the soil and seed
 can praise God
  who brings forth the fruit.
Office workers who mingle with the masses
  that impersonally jostle them
 and work amid the tall structures
  that belittle them
 can praise God who knows
  and loves them forever.
Without our God to praise and worship and serve,
 there is no real purpose in life,
  no meaning, no identity, and no reason
   for existing in this cold, calculating world.
You who are on beds of pain,
 even you have reason to praise the Lord.
You who are left to die in homes for the aged,
 you, too, can find purpose
  in praising the Lord.

When you feel you are forgotten,
 your loving God never forgets.
When you are tired and lonely,
 your great God will never leave your side.

Those people who have no God to praise,
 who neglect to come before
  their Creator and Redeemer,
 are like creatures wandering in darkness.
They focus on the fitful, fleeing things
 of this life.
Like butterflies over a flower bed,
 they flutter from blossom to blossom,
  getting their pollen wherever they can.
Then they return to their beds
 only to await the meaningless existence
  of another day.

God is available—to be recognized and praised.
He has reached out to His lost children
 to lovingly draw them to Himself.
He gives them identity and purpose,
 a name and a goal,
 and makes them
  eternally secure and significant.

Let us praise the Lord!
He makes our lives and our living,
 every hour and every day, truly worthwhile;
 and we belong to Him forever.

Thank You, God,
for all these things that reveal Your love.
Thank You for the heavens that cover us,
for the earth beneath our feet,
for the sun in the day and the stars in the night,
for the snow and the rains,
for mountains and valleys and trees and flowers.

Thank You, God,
for those people who demonstrate Your love.
Thank You for those great men and women who
followed You throughout history,
for the priests and prophets
and apostles and ministers,
for doctors and teachers and mothers and fathers
and painters and musicians and writers
and farmers and laborers and clerks,
for those men and women who gloried in Your love
and dedicated their lives
to loving others.

Thank You, God,
for choosing me to be one of Your people,
for calling me and equipping me to communicate
Your love to the world around me.
Thank You, God.

How grateful we are, O God,
for our great country
for the blessings You lavish on our land.
How concerned we are, O Lord,
that our nation may become our god
and that we worship the gifts
rather than the Giver!

Is it possible, O God,
that our laws may circumvent Your will?
that our freedom may place chains on others?
that our wealth may impoverish someone?
that our power may come
at the expense of another's weakness?
that our enemies may be those
who are obedient to You?

Dare we pray, O God,
that You take away those things that come
between us and You?
that You raise up men and women who will oppose
those institutions and those citizens
who carelessly, even unconsciously,
equate patriotism with allegiance to You?

We pray, O God,
that our nation may be restored to Your objectives
and that Your children who live in this land
may dedicate their lives to You and Your purposes.

138

I am exceedingly grateful, O Lord,
   for You have heard my cries and complaints,
   and You responded with mercy and strength.
Now my life is overflowing with thanksgiving,
   and my mouth is filled with Your praises.

If only the leaders of our disjointed world
      would listen to Your words
      and direct their people in accord with Your will.
Then they would know the meaning of peace,
   and they would rejoice in the ways of God.

You have not shielded me
      from the pains of trouble
         or the ravages of conflict,
      but You have kept me
         even amid sorrow and suffering.
You take my side against the enemies of my soul,
   and You will not allow them to destroy me.

Thus I know You will fulfill Your purpose for my life.
Your love and mercy are everlasting;
   You will not let me go.

O God, You know me inside and out,
 through and through.
Everything I do,
  every thought that flits through my mind,
  every step I take,
  every plan I make,
  every word I speak,
  You know, even before these things happen.
You know my past;
  You know my future.
Your enveloping presence covers my every move.
Your knowledge of me sometimes comforts me,
  sometimes frightens me,
  but it is always far beyond my comprehension.

There is no way to escape You, no place to hide.
If I ascend to the heights of joy,
  You are there before me.
If I plunge into the depths of despair,
  You are there to meet me.
I could fly to the other side of the world
  and find You there to lead the way.
I could walk into the darkest night,
  only to find You there
   to lighten its dismal hours.

You were present at my conception.
You guided the molding of my unformed members

within the body of my mother.
Nothing about me, from beginning to end,
    has been hidden from Your eyes.
How frightfully, fantastically wonderful it all is!

May Your all-knowing, everywhere-present Spirit
    continue to search out my feelings and thoughts.
Deliver me
       from that which may hurt or destroy me,
    and guide me along the paths of love and truth.

O God, deliver our nation and our world
from those people in positions of authority
who resort to violence
to carry out their objectives.
They sweet-talk us into believing
they are acting in our interests
and brainwash us into blind,
flag-waving allegiance
until we march by their side
into battles that destroy
our unity and joy as members of
the human family.

Deliver all of us, O Lord,
from the notion that anything of value or worth
can be obtained by hostile or violent actions.

Our God is on the side of those who are afflicted.
He will deal justly with people who are violent,
and show His mercy to the victims
of their obscene actions.

Help us, O Lord,
even at the risk of our lives and well-being,
to overcome hate with love
and to be peacemakers in a world
that is so racked and distorted
by the atrocities of violence.

141

O God, I come to You in sorrow and shame.
I spoke up in my own defense today
   and uttered words that knifed their way
      into the heart of my friend,
   and this created a great rift between us.
I would never raise my hand to strike anybody,
      but the tongue is more destructive than the fist,
      and I hurt the one I love.

Heal the hurt of my friend, O Lord,
      and heal the sickness within my heart
         that forced my foolish tongue
         into such irresponsible actions.

I come to claim Your loving mercy.
I pray, as well, that you grant my friend
      the grace to forgive me.
May Your Spirit who abides in my heart
      curb and control my rebellious tongue
      and teach me to speak words
         that give life and promote love
         in this hate-ridden world.

I direct my cries to the Lord.
Out of the ear-piercing sounds and
        ceaseless turmoil of this concrete jungle,
    I speak God's name.
For my heart is deeply troubled and depressed,
        and I feel weary and faint.

I am confused and lost.
I cannot find my way.
The nameless faces that flit by
        take no notice of me.
No one knows my name,
        and no one cares.

I turn to You, O God.
You have heard me before,
        and You responded to my cries.
Perhaps even amid the frustrating activity
        and crowded streets of this great land,
    You can hear the cries of a lonely child.

O God, deliver me from my prison of loneliness.
Turn my cries of distress
        into proclamations of joy.
Direct my steps into the fellowship
        of others who love and serve You.

143

It was another one of those days, Lord,
    when I should have stayed in bed.
Everything I attempted to do was headed for failure.
I honestly tried to show concern for others,
    but I got cold shoulders in return.
I tried to speak words of comfort,
    and they were thrown back into my teeth.
I wanted to do well at my job,
    but it seemed I just got in everybody's way.

Sometimes it just isn't worth it, Lord,
    and I wonder if it isn't time to fold up
        and shove off in search of greener pastures.
I want desperately to be a success,
    to add points to my score,
    or to get commended now and then.
But this didn't happen today, Lord,
    and it happens so seldom, I wonder what's wrong.
Am I following Your course for my life,
    or am I just muddling through
        without purpose or design?

I need You, God, now more than ever before.
And if I don't get some special lift,
        some sense of Your support and encouragement,
    I will go right down the tube.

Come closer, O Lord, that I may hear again
    Your voice of comfort and concern.

144

$\mathcal{O}$ *God, it is difficult to understand*
how You can hold Your creatures in such high regard
and show them such concern.
Their years on this earth are so few.
They are little more than a wisp of wind
in the time and space of Your great universe.

You created them as the objects of Your love—
only to see them turn from You
to play with their foolish toys.
You tried to teach them to love their fellow beings—
only to see them express
their fears and suspicion and hate
through cruel acts of violence and war.
You showered on them Your abundant gifts—
only to see them make these gifts their
ultimate concern.

Still You continue to love them
and seek continuously to save them
from destroying themselves and the world
You have placed in their hands.
Even while they reject You,
You reach out to draw them back to Yourself.
Even while they suffer the painful consequences
of rank rebelliousness,
You offer to them Your healing
and demonstrate Your desire
to restore them to love and joy.

And when they finally turn to You,
    they find You waiting for them,
        ready to forgive their sins and to welcome them
        to Your life and purposes once more.

Those who return to their Lord are happy indeed!
They will forever be the objects
    of God's love and blessings.

God is here—let's celebrate!

Let us enlist our lives in continuous celebration
    of God's goodness and greatness.
Let us announce to the world God's presence
    and proclaim His loving concern for all His creatures.
How compassionate He is toward all He has created,
    how tender toward His failure-fraught creatures!
He will not back out on His promises to us.
His blessings are not reserved only for those
    who fit obediently into His design for them.
He is just—and He is forgiving.
He gently picks up those who have fallen
    and restores them to Himself.
He sustains those who are wavering in weakness
    and grants them His grace and strength.
He reaches into the void of empty lives
    and enriches and fulfills their hungry hearts.
He is near enough to hear our every cry,
    to sense our every need,
      to grant us whatever is necessary
    to make us happy and productive
      as we seek to follow and to serve Him.

How incomparably glorious is our great God!
May our mouths articulate and our lives demonstrate
    His ever-present love for all His creatures!
Let us celebrate
    the eternal mercy and goodness of our God!

Praise God!
As long as I have breath in my body,
    I will praise God!

Don't pin your hopes on the genius of men or women.
Their ultimate end is the same as yours,
    and they become once more
        like the dust from which they came.

Those who draw their strength from God are secure.
He who created the earth and all upon it
    is the only One who can heal the wounds
    and mend the fractures of our disjointed world.
He can break the bonds of obsession
    and pierce humanity's stupor with visions of truth.
He tenderly reaches out
        to those who are oppressed
    and reveals His concern
        for those who are lost and lonely.
He watches over His own
    while the paths of the godless
        lead to their own destruction.

This is the God who cannot die!
Praise God!
Amen!

*H*ow good it is to celebrate God's presence
and to sing His praises throughout each day!
We celebrate what He has done for His children
through history:
His creation of our world
and the sun and the moon and
the unnumbered stars
that light up our universe;
His creatures that swim and crawl
and walk and fly on our planet;
His children chosen to enjoy
these great gifts around them.
We praise Him for dealing with His human creatures
through His blessings heaped upon them;
His revelations through signs and wonders;
His tender love and gentle concern
in His care shown toward them.
We praise Him for His devoted servants:
who communicated His Word;
who performed His miracles;
who brought His healing to people's hurts.
We celebrate His continued blessings to our world:
the flowers that bloom in glorious color;
the rains that freshen the earth;
the birds that fill the air with song.

We give thanks for His perpetual love:
His forgiveness of our sins;

His pursuit of those who run from Him;
His reaching out to heal them
and to draw them to Himself.

We call all men and women to praise the Lord:
    those who preach to proclaim His love;
    those who sing to glorify His name;
    those who can shout or whistle
        or write or paint
        or dance or play musical instruments
    or pound on drums or ring bells
        to join in celebrating
    the majesty of our great and loving God.